1

MODERN CEO TOOLKIT

MODERN CEO TOOLKIT

Winning Tips for Career Success

DARRIN ELFORD

DARRIN ELFORD
PREMIUM BOOKS

ISBN: 978-1-991363-03-9 (Paperback)

eISBN: 978-1-991363-04-6 (E-Book)

First edition

About the Author

Darrin is a seasoned business leader with over two decades of experience in guiding companies toward growth, innovation, and success. Having held leadership roles across various industries, Darrin has a proven track record of helping executives and entrepreneurs navigate the complexities of modern business.

Throughout his career, Darrin has worked with startups and established corporations alike, developing strategies for scaling businesses, building high-performance teams, implementing operational excellence programs and embracing change. His expertise extends to leadership, corporate governance, financial management, and fostering organizational cultures that prioritize innovation and corporate growth.

A passionate advocate for continuous learning, Darrin has mentored countless executives and emerging leaders. His approach to leadership is rooted in emotional intelligence, resilience, and the belief that great leaders are also great learners. Drawing from real-world experiences, Darrin brings a practical, actionable perspective to every lesson shared in this book.

When not consulting or leading companies to success, Darrin enjoys spending time with his family, exploring new technologies, and contributing to initiatives that foster diversity, equity, and inclusion in business.

Acknowledgements

Writing this book has been a journey filled with insights, growth, and the support of many incredible people. First and foremost, I want to thank the executive leaders in my life - past and present - who have inspired me to dive deeper into the dynamics of being a successful CEO. Your challenges, feedback, and wisdom have been invaluable in shaping the ideas I share here.

To my readers: thank you for picking up this book. You're already taking the first step towards becoming a better, more confident CEO in your chosen sector. I hope the tools and insights within these pages empower you to understand yourself, hone your skills and become the effective leader you were meant to be.

I also want to express my deepest gratitude to my loved ones who helped turn my ideas into a structured, coherent, and readable book. Your hard work and patience have made this possible, and for that, I am truly grateful.

To my mentors: your guidance, support, and encouragement have shaped my career and helped me refine the concepts I teach. Your influence has been a key part of my growth as both a writer and a teacher.

Finally, to the countless peers and executive leaders who have shared their personal experiences with me over the years, thank you. Your stories and struggles have been the fuel for my understanding of this subject, and I am honored to have learned from each of you.

This book wouldn't have been possible without all of you. Thank you for your wisdom, your trust, and your unwavering support.

Table of Contents

Introduction

Becoming a successful CEO is more than just holding a title or managing a company's bottom line. It's about shaping the future, inspiring your team, navigating challenges, and making decisions that will resonate for years to come. In *Modern CEO Toolkit* I share the principles, insights, and strategies that have helped me—and countless other leaders—thrive in today's fast-paced, ever-changing business world.

In this book, you will find the essential qualities that define great CEOs: resilience, emotional intelligence, strategic vision, and the ability to foster a culture of growth and excellence. You'll learn how to navigate the complexities of modern business, from building high-performance teams and mastering financial literacy, to embracing technology and leading with ethical values.

Each lesson is drawn from real-life experiences, case studies, and practical strategies that you can implement immediately to transform both your leadership and your organization. Whether you're at the beginning of your leadership journey or an experienced CEO seeking to refine your approach, this book offers valuable tools to help you thrive.

As a CEO, your decisions shape not only the future of your company but also the lives of the people who rely on your leadership. In the pages that follow, I will guide you through the core competencies that every successful CEO must master, offering a clear roadmap for building a resilient, innovative, and high-performing organization.

The journey of leadership is never easy, but it's one that brings incredible rewards. I invite you to take the lessons in this book, apply them in your own way, and make your mark as a leader who drives lasting success.

Welcome to *Modern CEO Toolkit*—let's get started on your journey to greatness.

Darrin Elford
Certified Chief Executive Officer

1

The Mindset of a Successful CEO

The difference between a good CEO and a great one often lies in their mindset. It's not just about the decisions they make, but how they think, how they approach challenges, and how they view the world. The mindset of a successful CEO is one that embraces growth, innovation, and resilience. It shapes their actions, fuels their passion, and influences how they lead their teams.

In this chapter, we'll explore the key elements of the CEO mindset—how top leaders think, how they approach obstacles, and how you can develop this mindset for yourself. Let's break down the core components that make up the mindset of a successful CEO.

1. Growth-Oriented Thinking: Always Evolving

A successful CEO has a growth mindset. This means they are always looking for opportunities to learn, evolve, and improve—both personally and professionally. They don't rest on their laurels or become complacent with success. Instead, they continuously seek ways to improve their leadership, refine their strategies, and adapt to changing circumstances.

Great CEOs see challenges as opportunities to grow, not as setbacks. When things go wrong, they ask themselves, *What can I learn from this?* They are never "done" learning. Whether it's through reading books, attending seminars, seeking feedback from others, or even learning from failures, they are committed to constant development.

Action

Embrace a mindset of continuous learning. Set aside time every week to read industry reports, listen to leadership podcasts, or attend webinars. Seek feedback from your team on your leadership and find one area to improve each quarter. The more you learn, the better equipped you'll be to make strategic decisions and lead with confidence.

2. Visionary Thinking: Seeing Beyond the Now

One of the defining characteristics of a successful CEO is their ability to see the big picture. They don't just focus on today's problems or tomorrow's tasks—they think in terms of years or even decades ahead. Successful CEOs are visionaries who create and nurture a compelling vision of the future, and they inspire their teams to pursue it.

This visionary mindset allows them to spot trends, anticipate market shifts, and position their companies ahead of competitors. They're not simply reacting to the present—they are creating the future.

Action

Develop a long-term vision for your company. Look beyond the next quarter or fiscal year and ask, *Where do I want this company to be in five years?* Once you've defined that vision, share it with your team and get everyone on board. Constantly remind yourself and your team of the big picture and align your daily actions with that long-term goal.

3. Resilience: Bouncing Back Stronger

In the fast-paced, ever-changing world of business, setbacks are inevitable. Whether it's a missed deadline, a failed product launch, or an economic downturn, challenges will come. What sets successful CEOs apart is their ability to stay resilient in the face of adversity.

They don't allow failure to define them; instead, they see it as a stepping stone toward success. They remain calm under pressure, adapt to new circumstances, and bounce back stronger than before. Resilient CEOs know that setbacks are part of the journey, and they maintain a positive, solution-focused mindset even when things get tough.

Action

Build your resilience by reframing setbacks as learning opportunities. Instead of dwelling on mistakes, ask yourself what you can take away from them. Surround yourself with a support system of mentors, peers, or coaches who can help you stay grounded and focused when challenges arise. Practice mindfulness or stress-relief techniques to help you stay calm under pressure.

4. Decisiveness: Trusting Your Judgement

One of the key traits of a successful CEO is decisiveness. They make decisions quickly, even when there's uncertainty. While they gather the necessary information and weigh the pros and cons, they don't get paralyzed by the fear of making a mistake. Successful CEOs trust their instincts and make the best possible decisions with the information at hand.

Decisiveness isn't about always being right—it's about taking action. A successful CEO knows that delaying decisions can lead to missed opportunities. They set a clear course and take steps toward that goal, adjusting along the way if needed.

Action

Practice making decisions more quickly. Start by setting small, low-stakes decisions for yourself, and then gradually work your way up to bigger, more impactful choices. Trust your judgment and commit to your decisions. Don't let fear of failure slow you down—decisive action is often better than no action at all.

5. Optimism: Keeping the Faith

Successful CEOs are naturally optimistic. This doesn't mean they ignore reality or deny challenges, but they have an unwavering belief that success is possible. Optimism is about maintaining a positive outlook and seeing potential where others may see obstacles. It's about focusing on solutions rather than problems, and about believing that the future can be better than the present.

This optimism is contagious. When a CEO is optimistic, it spreads throughout the organization, boosting morale and driving employees to work harder toward common goals. Optimism helps CEOs stay motivated during tough times, and it allows them to inspire and energize their teams.

Action

Cultivate a positive mindset by practicing gratitude. Every day, write down three things you are grateful for. Focus on the positives, even in difficult situations, and share your optimism with your team. When you face challenges, maintain a solution-oriented approach and encourage others to do the same.

6. Adaptability: Navigating Change with Ease

The business world is constantly evolving. New technologies, market dynamics, and customer preferences can all shift unexpectedly. Successful CEOs are adaptable—they thrive in change, rather than resisting it. They embrace new ideas and are open to rethinking their strategies when necessary. They know that the ability to pivot quickly is crucial for long-term success.

Adaptability is not just about reacting to changes, but also about proactively seeking out new ways to innovate and improve. CEOs with this mindset are always looking for opportunities to improve their business and stay ahead of the competition.

Action

Stay flexible and open to change. Regularly assess your strategies and be willing to adjust when new information or challenges arise. Encourage a culture of adaptability within your team by rewarding innovative thinking and creating an environment where new ideas are welcome.

7. Empathy: Understanding Others' Perspectives

Successful CEOs are empathetic. They understand the needs and concerns of their employees, customers, and partners. This empathy allows them to build strong relationships and create a positive organizational culture. By listening to others, they make informed decisions that consider the broader impact on people.

Empathy is not about sympathy, but about understanding. It helps CEOs connect with others on a deeper level, earn trust, and inspire loyalty. Employees who feel heard and valued are more likely to be motivated and engaged.

Action

Practice active listening in all your interactions. Pay attention to what people are saying (and not saying), and ask thoughtful questions to gain a deeper understanding of their perspectives. Show appreciation for others' ideas and concerns and incorporate their feedback into your decision-making.

Conclusion: Shaping Your CEO Mindset

The mindset of a successful CEO is a powerful tool. It shapes how they respond to challenges, how they inspire their teams, and how they drive their companies toward success. By cultivating a growth-oriented mindset, embracing resilience, practicing decisiveness, staying optimistic, adapting to change, and leading with empathy, you can begin to develop the mindset necessary to thrive as a CEO.

Remember, the CEO mindset isn't something you either have or don't have—it's something that can be developed over time. The more you nurture these qualities, the more naturally they will come to you. By committing to this mindset, you are not just leading your company—you are leading yourself toward greater success and fulfilment.

Case Study: Emily Davis – CEO of GreenLeaf Solutions

Emily Davis, the CEO of GreenLeaf Solutions, a fast-growing company focused on providing sustainable energy solutions, faced a pivotal moment in her leadership journey. When she took over as CEO, GreenLeaf was a solid business, but it had plateaued. While the company was respected in the renewable energy industry, it wasn't growing as quickly as competitors. In an industry driven by constant innovation and change, Emily knew that to succeed, she had to lead her company with the right mindset.

In this case study, we'll explore how Emily's mindset helped her transform GreenLeaf Solutions and positioned the company as a leader in the sustainable energy space.

1. Growth-Oriented Thinking: Relentlessly Pursuing Improvement

Emily believed that to lead her company forward, she first needed to cultivate a mindset of growth—both for herself and her team. She spent the first few months as CEO getting to know her employees, understanding their strengths, and identifying areas where they could improve. Emily wasn't content with the status quo. She encouraged her team to learn new skills, attend workshops, and explore ideas outside their typical scope of work.

She herself became a student of leadership. Emily read books on strategy, attended industry conferences, and sought feedback from mentors. She recognized that to inspire her team, she needed to show them that learning was a constant process.

Real-World Example: Emily launched a monthly "learning lunch" initiative where different employees could present new ideas or industry trends. This not only encouraged a growth mindset across the company but also gave employees a platform to share innovative ideas they were excited about.

Key Takeaway:

Emily's commitment to continuous learning helped foster a culture of improvement. By promoting growth-oriented thinking, she set the stage for GreenLeaf Solutions to innovate and evolve.

2. Visionary Thinking: Setting a Bold Direction

When Emily first evaluated GreenLeaf Solutions, she quickly realized that while the company was providing quality products, it lacked a compelling long-term vision. Competitors were pushing boundaries with new technology, and the market was becoming increasingly competitive. Emily knew that to stay relevant, she needed to cast a bold vision for the future.

Emily's vision was clear: she wanted GreenLeaf Solutions to become a leader in smart, sustainable energy systems—integrating AI and IoT (Internet of Things) into renewable energy management. She saw a future where every home and business could optimize energy use with minimal environmental impact.

But Emily didn't just have a vision; she communicated it constantly. During company meetings, she spoke about this vision, bringing the team along and aligning every project and decision with this future-focused goal. Emily's ability to create and communicate a clear vision became a driving force that aligned everyone at GreenLeaf Solutions.

Real-World Example: Emily invited key stakeholders, including customers and employees, to vision-setting workshops. By involving them in the visioning process, she created a sense of ownership, and the team became more passionate about achieving the company's ambitious goals.

3. Resilience: Navigating Setbacks

In the second year of Emily's leadership, GreenLeaf Solutions faced a major challenge. A new competitor entered the market with a similar product, but at a lower price. This threatened the company's market share, and Emily knew they had to act fast. However, her first reaction wasn't panic—it was to take a deep breath and focus on the bigger picture.

Rather than immediately lowering prices, Emily led her team to focus on enhancing their product with smarter features, offering superior customer service, and creating partnerships with eco-conscious brands. She reinforced the importance of resilience, telling her team, *"We're not here to follow others; we're here to set the standard."* Emily also ensured that during this stressful time, the team maintained a positive attitude and kept the focus on what they could control.

Real-World Example: Emily's response to the competition was a series of internal brainstorming sessions. She encouraged her team to think creatively about how to differentiate GreenLeaf Solutions—not just with pricing, but through unique, innovative features that showcased the company's values.

4. Decisiveness: Quick and Confident Decision-Making

The challenge Emily faced with the new competitor required quick action. She didn't have time to gather endless data or overthink the situation. Instead, she trusted her instincts and made a firm decision: GreenLeaf Solutions would double down on customer experience and integrate cutting-edge technology into their products. Emily made it clear to her team that they would focus on innovation and improving the customer experience, rather than engaging in a price war.

Her decisiveness inspired confidence across the organization. Employees knew exactly where the company was headed, and they understood their role in executing the new strategy.

Real-World Example: Emily organized a task force to develop a new product feature within three months. She gave them clear goals and timelines, empowering the team to take action without waiting for lengthy approval processes.

Key Takeaway:

Emily's ability to make clear, confident decisions helped GreenLeaf Solutions stay focused and move quickly during a period of uncertainty. Her decisive leadership prevented the company from being bogged down by indecision or fear.

5. Optimism: Leading with a Positive Outlook

Despite the challenges GreenLeaf Solutions faced, Emily remained an optimist. She understood that uncertainty was part of the business landscape, and while problems were inevitable, they could always be solved. She communicated this optimism to her team, consistently reinforcing that challenges were opportunities to innovate and grow.

Her positive attitude had a profound impact on company morale. During tough moments, when the pressure was high, Emily encouraged her team to focus on the solutions rather than dwell on the problems. She celebrated small wins, knowing that those moments of success would fuel the momentum needed to push through bigger challenges.

Real-World Example: When the competitor's product initially gained traction, Emily gathered her team for a celebratory event. Rather than focusing on the competition, she highlighted the unique strengths of GreenLeaf's approach, leaving the team feeling proud of their work.

Key Takeaway:

Emily's optimism helped create a resilient culture at GreenLeaf Solutions. Her belief in the company's success and her ability to maintain a positive outlook, even during difficult times, was contagious.

6. Adaptability: Embracing Change

As the renewable energy market shifted, with new technologies constantly emerging, Emily made adaptability a core value of GreenLeaf Solutions. She encouraged her team to be flexible and open to change, ensuring that innovation was always at the forefront of their work.

When the market began to demand more eco-friendly solutions, Emily quickly pivoted the company's focus to more energy-efficient products. She also ensured that her team was constantly updating their skills to stay competitive in an industry that was rapidly evolving.

Real-World Example: Emily supported the launch of a new product line that incorporated solar energy with smart home technology. She recognized that the future of energy would involve integration, and GreenLeaf's adaptability allowed them to stay ahead of the curve.

Key Takeaway:

Emily's adaptability allowed GreenLeaf Solutions to stay relevant and competitive, even as the market changed. She fostered a culture that embraced change as an opportunity for growth.

7. Empathy: Connecting with People

Throughout her journey, Emily demonstrated empathy in every aspect of her leadership. She listened to her employees' concerns, celebrated their achievements, and ensured they felt valued. She knew that a company's success wasn't just about the bottom line—it was about the people driving that success.

When GreenLeaf Solutions faced its toughest moments, Emily made sure to spend time with her team, offering support and listening to their ideas. She encouraged open dialogue, ensuring that everyone's voice was heard.

Real-World Example: Emily hosted monthly "open-door" sessions where employees could share feedback, ask questions, or express concerns. This open communication helped her stay connected with the team and fostered trust throughout the company.

Key Takeaway:

Emily's empathy strengthened the company culture. By truly understanding her team's perspectives, she built trust and loyalty, making her team more engaged and motivated to achieve company goals.

Conclusion: Emily's CEO Mindset in Action

Emily Davis' success as CEO of GreenLeaf Solutions is a powerful example of how mindset shapes leadership. Through growth-oriented thinking, visionary leadership, resilience, decisiveness, optimism, adaptability, and empathy, Emily not only led her company to success but also created a thriving organizational culture.

For any CEO or aspiring leader, Emily's approach demonstrates that leadership is not just about making the right decisions—it's about cultivating the right mindset. By adopting these principles, you can lead your company to new heights, no matter the challenges you face.

2

Professional Qualities of a CEO

The role of a CEO is not merely one of oversight but one of leadership, vision, and influence. Whether you're at the helm of a startup or managing a multinational corporation, the qualities that define a successful CEO are both learned and honed. In this chapter, we will explore the core attributes that distinguish great CEOs, offering a roadmap for those who aspire to not only lead but thrive in the most demanding executive role.

1. Visionary Thinking

At the heart of every great CEO is a visionary mindset. Vision is not simply about anticipating the future; it is about shaping it. A successful CEO must possess the ability to see beyond the horizon and chart a course that inspires innovation and progress. This requires an understanding of industry trends, a keen sense of emerging technologies, and, perhaps most importantly, a bold imagination that can transform an organization from where it is to where it could be.

The visionary CEO does not simply react to changes in the market; they anticipate them. They foresee the needs of tomorrow's customer, the disruption of the current business model, and the potential for innovation in ways that others cannot yet fathom. Cultivating this mindset involves not only seeking knowledge but also fostering a culture of forward-thinking in the organization. It is the responsibility of the CEO to paint a compelling picture of the future that motivates and unites the entire company toward a common goal.

2. Decisive Leadership

Decisiveness is another cornerstone of effective leadership. The pace of business today is relentless, and hesitation is often the greatest enemy of success.

CEOs are faced with constant, high-stakes decisions—from strategic acquisitions to product launches, from personnel changes to financial investments. The ability to make decisions swiftly and confidently, even in the face of uncertainty, separates top-tier leaders from the rest.

However, decisiveness should never be mistaken for rashness. A successful CEO knows that while speed is important, decisions must be informed. This requires gathering the right data, consulting with key stakeholders, and weighing potential risks and rewards. But in the end, the leader must trust their judgment and make choices that are in alignment with the company's long-term objectives.

Developing this quality comes down to experience, intuition, and emotional intelligence. It involves understanding that inaction can be as detrimental as a poor decision and learning to embrace the discomfort that comes with taking risks.

3. Resilience in the Face of Adversity

Leadership at the highest level is often a battle of attrition. Challenges will arise—economic downturns, industry shifts, internal strife, and market competition. The successful CEO is one who thrives in adversity, emerging stronger after each setback.

Resilience is not just about bouncing back; it's about learning and evolving from each challenge. The greatest leaders are those who can maintain composure and focus during times of crisis. They are strategic in their response, ensuring that the organization emerges not only intact but better prepared for future challenges.

This quality is often developed through experience, though it can be nurtured through deliberate practices such as mindfulness, stress management, and emotional regulation. CEOs must lead by example during turbulent times, showing their teams that setbacks are not failures but opportunities for growth.

4. Emotional Intelligence (EQ)

Emotional intelligence (EQ) is one of the most significant differentiators between average and exceptional leaders. As the face of the organization, the CEO must manage a broad spectrum of emotions—from those of their employees to those of customers, investors, and partners. The ability to empathize, communicate effectively, and navigate complex interpersonal dynamics is a skill that top-tier CEOs cultivate deliberately.

Emotional intelligence begins with self-awareness—the capacity to understand one's own emotions and how they affect decisions and relationships. It extends to social awareness, the ability to read the emotions of others, and the adaptability to respond appropriately in any situation. A CEO who exhibits high EQ can build trust, foster collaboration, and drive a culture of respect and inclusivity.

In practice, developing emotional intelligence requires ongoing self-reflection, active listening, and seeking feedback. CEOs should also invest in building relationships across all levels of the organization, ensuring they are in touch with the pulse of the business and the people who drive its success.

5. Strategic Agility

The business world is in constant flux, with new challenges, opportunities, and competitors emerging at a rapid pace. Successful CEOs must possess strategic agility—the ability to adapt quickly and effectively to changing circumstances while staying aligned with the company's overarching goals.

Strategic agility is not about reacting to every change in the environment but understanding when to pivot and how to align resources for maximum impact. It involves being proactive rather than simply responsive. Agility is about fostering a culture of flexibility within the organization, where innovation and new ideas are encouraged, and where the leadership is empowered to make adjustments as needed.

The key to developing strategic agility lies in continual learning and openness to new ideas. CEOs must stay abreast of industry developments, be willing to embrace unconventional solutions, and remain nimble enough to course-correct when necessary.

6. Effective Communication

The role of a CEO is, by nature, a communication-intensive one. Whether presenting to investors, speaking with employees, or engaging with customers, the CEO's ability to convey a clear, compelling message is paramount. Communication is not just about delivering information; it is about persuasion, motivation, and inspiring others to take action.

Effective communication goes beyond words. It involves body language, tone, timing, and the ability to listen as much as to speak. A successful CEO is one who can tailor their message to different audiences, creating alignment and fostering understanding at every level of the organization.

To develop this quality, CEOs should work on becoming more articulate, empathetic, and transparent. They must be able to communicate both the vision of the company and the path to achieving it, ensuring that every stakeholder feels included and motivated by the company's mission.

7. Integrity and Ethics

In an era where trust is increasingly hard to come by, integrity and ethical leadership are non-negotiable qualities for any CEO. The behavior of the CEO sets the tone for the entire organization, and a leader who prioritizes ethical decision-making will inspire confidence in both internal and external stakeholders.

Integrity is about consistency in word and deed. A CEO must model the values they wish to see in their organization and hold themselves to the highest standards of honesty, fairness, and accountability. Ethical leadership is not simply about avoiding scandals but about creating a culture where ethical behavior is ingrained in the company's DNA.

Developing integrity as a CEO involves making principled decisions even when it's difficult, standing firm in the face of pressure, and being transparent in all dealings. It requires the courage to uphold the organization's values, even when doing so might come at a personal or professional cost.

Conclusion: A Continuous Journey of Growth

The qualities of a successful CEO are not innate; they are cultivated over time through deliberate effort, experience, and reflection. Becoming a great leader involves not just managing a company but continually managing and developing oneself. By focusing on visionary thinking, decisiveness, resilience, emotional intelligence, strategic agility, communication, and integrity, a CEO can build the foundation for enduring success.

The journey to becoming a successful CEO is a marathon, not a sprint. It requires a commitment to personal growth and an unwavering dedication to the organization's mission. With these qualities as the pillars of leadership, the modern CEO will not only guide their company to success but inspire a new generation of leaders to follow in their footsteps.

Practical Actionable Steps to Develop the 7 Essential Qualities of a Successful CEO

Now that we've explored the key qualities of a successful CEO, it's time to break them down into actionable steps you can take to develop these attributes in your own leadership journey. Becoming a great CEO isn't a destination, but a process—a continuous journey of learning, adapting, and refining your skills. Here are the practical steps you can implement immediately to start building the seven qualities that will set you apart as a successful leader.

1. Visionary Thinking: Cultivate a Future-Oriented Mindset

- **Step 1: Set Time for Strategic Reflection** – Dedicate at least one hour every week to think deeply about the future of your industry, your company, and your personal goals. Ask yourself: *Where do I want to be in 5 years? What are the emerging trends in my field? What challenges or opportunities can we foresee?* Document your thoughts and review them regularly to refine your vision.

- **Step 2: Encourage Innovation** – Create an environment where new ideas are welcomed. Regularly ask your team for input on how to innovate or improve your products, services, or internal processes. Set up brainstorming sessions or innovation workshops to stimulate creative thinking.

- **Step 3: Read Widely** – Read books, articles, and case studies from leaders across industries. The broader your understanding of business models and success stories, the clearer your own vision will become.

2. Decisive Leadership: Make Quick and Informed Decisions

- **Step 1: Build a Framework for Decision-Making** – Develop a process to evaluate decisions quickly. This could include outlining key criteria (cost, impact, time frame, etc.) for making strategic calls. By having a system, you reduce the mental clutter and improve your decision-making speed.

- **Step 2: Don't Fear Mistakes** – Accept that not every decision will be perfect. The key is learning from mistakes and adjusting your strategy. Start small if necessary, but always be ready to act when the situation calls for it.

- **Step 3: Delegate When Appropriate** – Remember, you don't need to make every decision yourself. Empower your team members with the authority to make decisions within their scope of responsibility. This not only frees up your time but also helps develop leadership across your organization.

3. Resilience in the Face of Adversity: Build Mental Toughness

- **Step 1: Embrace Challenges as Opportunities** – Reframe setbacks as learning opportunities. When faced with failure, ask yourself, *What can I learn from this?* Rather than focusing on the negative, identify one lesson you can take from each challenge.

- **Step 2: Practice Self-Care** – Mental resilience is supported by physical well-being. Ensure that you are managing stress through exercise, adequate sleep, and relaxation techniques such as meditation or mindfulness.

- **Step 3: Create a Support Network** – Build relationships with other leaders, mentors, or peer groups who can provide perspective and advice when you face tough situations. Surrounding yourself with trusted advisors can make a huge difference during turbulent times.

4. Emotional Intelligence (EQ): Understand Yourself and Others

- **Step 1: Practice Active Listening** – When communicating with others, focus fully on listening rather than just responding. This builds empathy and helps you understand the emotions and needs of others. Give your full attention, ask clarifying questions, and show you value their perspective.

- **Step 2: Reflect on Your Own Emotions** – Develop self-awareness by regularly reflecting on how you react emotionally to different situations. Keep a journal where you write about your emotional responses to key events and decisions. This helps you recognize patterns and adjust your reactions.

- **Step 3: Provide Constructive Feedback** – Build emotional intelligence within your team by offering feedback that is constructive and empathetic. Approach difficult conversations with care, focusing on solutions rather than placing blame. This helps create an emotionally intelligent culture.

5. Strategic Agility: Adapt and Respond to Change

- **Step 1: Stay Informed** – Constantly monitor industry news, competitors, and technological advancements. Set up Google Alerts or subscribe to relevant journals and newsletters to stay ahead of trends that might impact your business.

- **Step 2: Set Contingency Plans** – For each major business decision, create backup plans. If a strategy doesn't go as expected, having a contingency plan allows you to pivot quickly without losing momentum.

- **Step 3: Be Open to Feedback** – Encourage a culture of openness, where feedback—especially critical feedback—is welcome. Regularly ask your employees, customers, and partners what you can do better. This will help you stay agile and make adjustments in real-time.

6. Effective Communication: Connect and Inspire

- **Step 1: Prioritize Clear Messaging** – Whether you're writing an email or giving a speech, always ensure your message is clear, concise, and aligned with your company's values. Avoid jargon and make your communication understandable for all audiences.

- **Step 2: Build Trust Through Transparency** – Foster open communication within your organization by sharing both successes and challenges. When you are transparent, your team is more likely to trust your leadership and feel engaged in the company's journey.

- **Step 3: Hone Your Public Speaking Skills** – Strong communication often involves public speaking. Take opportunities to practice speaking in front of groups—whether it's at company meetings, networking events, or industry conferences. The more you practice, the more confident and effective you'll become.

7. Integrity and Ethics: Lead with Character

- **Step 1: Define Your Core Values** – Take the time to clearly define your personal and organizational values. Write them down, share them with your team, and refer to them often when making decisions. By aligning your actions with these values, you'll demonstrate consistency in leadership.

- **Step 2: Hold Yourself Accountable** – As the CEO, you set the tone. Hold yourself accountable to the same standards you expect from your team. Lead by example and be transparent about mistakes or challenges you face.

- **Step 3: Create an Ethical Framework for Your Team** – Establish a clear code of conduct within your organization. Provide regular training on ethical behavior and ensure that all employees, at every level, are aligned with the company's ethical standards. When people see you prioritize ethics, they will follow suit.

Conclusion: Taking Action Today for a Stronger Tomorrow

These actionable steps are not one-time tasks but practices to be woven into your daily routine. Developing the qualities of a successful CEO requires consistent effort and a commitment to growth. Implement these strategies with purpose, and you will begin to see real transformation not only in your leadership but in the overall success of your organization.

Remember, leadership is a journey, not a destination. By focusing on continuous improvement and making deliberate efforts to cultivate these seven qualities, you will create a lasting impact that will resonate across your company, industry, and beyond.

Case Study: Sarah Thomas – CEO of InnovateTech

Sarah Thomas had always been passionate about technology. After working her way up through the ranks of various tech companies, she finally had the opportunity to lead her own startup, InnovateTech, a small software development firm focused on creating cutting-edge solutions for the healthcare industry. When Sarah took over as CEO, InnovateTech was struggling. The company was losing market share, facing fierce competition, and morale was low. But over the next few years, Sarah transformed InnovateTech into a highly successful, profitable business with a reputation for innovation and exceptional service. Her leadership style became a powerful example of the seven qualities of a successful CEO.

1. Visionary Thinking: Seeing Beyond the Horizon

From the moment Sarah stepped into the CEO role, she knew the company needed a new direction. InnovateTech's primary product was a healthcare management system that wasn't gaining traction in the market. Sarah understood that the healthcare industry was on the brink of a digital revolution, with artificial intelligence (AI) and machine learning poised to transform patient care.

She set a bold vision to reposition InnovateTech as a leader in AI-driven healthcare solutions. Sarah didn't just envision the company's future; she communicated this vision to the entire team in a way that inspired them. She held a series of meetings where she explained how AI could revolutionize patient outcomes and how InnovateTech could play a central role in that transformation. Employees who had been uncertain about the future suddenly felt a renewed sense of purpose.

Practical Step:

Sarah made time every week to research emerging technologies, industry shifts, and potential future trends. By staying ahead of the curve, she ensured that InnovateTech wasn't just reacting to changes—it was shaping them.

2. Decisive Leadership: Acting Quickly and Confidently

Within the first few months, Sarah faced a critical decision: whether to continue developing their current product, which had limited potential, or pivot to an entirely new AI-based healthcare solution. The decision was tough, but Sarah knew that hesitation would only cost the company more time and money.

She consulted with key members of the team, analyzed market data, and made a decisive call to pivot. The decision was risky, but Sarah's confidence in the new direction gave the team the courage to follow her lead.

Practical Step:

Sarah trusted her gut while balancing it with data and feedback from her team. She didn't overthink the decision but acted swiftly, making it clear to the company that decisive leadership was expected at all levels.

3. Resilience in the Face of Adversity: Bouncing Back from Setbacks

As InnovateTech began the process of developing their new AI-driven product, they faced multiple setbacks. The development took longer than anticipated, key partnerships fell through, and an early prototype of the product had significant flaws. The pressure mounted, but Sarah remained calm and focused.

Rather than letting the setbacks derail the team, she used them as learning opportunities. She encouraged her employees to embrace failure as a part of the innovation process. "We're not here to avoid mistakes, but to learn from them and adapt," she often told them.

Practical Step:

Sarah led by example, showing resilience by working tirelessly through difficult moments. She acknowledged the challenges but always emphasized the importance of perseverance and adaptation.

4. Emotional Intelligence (EQ): Leading with Empathy and Understanding

One of Sarah's most valuable qualities was her emotional intelligence. She understood that leadership wasn't just about numbers and strategy—it was about people. She made a point of getting to know her employees, not just as workers but as individuals.

During tough times, Sarah would check in with her team members, asking how they were doing personally. She could sense when someone was feeling overwhelmed and would offer support or adjust workloads to help them manage stress. Her ability to connect with others on an emotional level created a strong sense of loyalty and trust within the company.

Practical Step:

Sarah scheduled regular one-on-ones with key team members. She actively listened to their concerns and provided personalized guidance, making them feel valued and heard.

5. Strategic Agility: Adapting to Market Changes

As InnovateTech moved forward with its new AI healthcare solution, the market continued to evolve. A major competitor released a similar product, and the regulatory landscape around AI in healthcare started to shift. Sarah knew she had to move quickly but also needed to ensure that InnovateTech was positioned to adapt to these changes.

Instead of reacting in a panic, Sarah quickly adjusted the product's features to meet new market demands. She also initiated discussions with legal experts to ensure the company remained compliant with emerging regulations. By staying flexible and responsive, InnovateTech was able to maintain its competitive edge.

Practical Step:

Sarah made it a point to regularly revisit the company's strategy in light of new developments in the market. She created a flexible plan that allowed InnovateTech to pivot without losing sight of its overall goals.

6. Effective Communication: Clear and Persuasive Messaging

Sarah understood the power of communication. As InnovateTech's new product neared launch, she knew that getting buy-in from both internal and external stakeholders would be crucial. She communicated the company's vision and progress clearly, regularly updating investors, customers, and employees on milestones.

Internally, Sarah encouraged an open-door policy, where employees felt comfortable sharing ideas and feedback. She also worked hard to ensure that everyone in the company understood how their work contributed to the larger vision, reinforcing the sense of purpose.

Practical Step:

Sarah held monthly town hall meetings to update the entire company on the status of projects and goals. She was transparent about challenges and successes, fostering an environment of trust and alignment.

7. Integrity and Ethics: Leading with Strong Values

Throughout her leadership, Sarah made sure that integrity was at the core of InnovateTech's culture. She was adamant about ethical practices, particularly when it came to the use of AI in healthcare. While many companies were focused solely on profitability, Sarah ensured that InnovateTech's solutions prioritized patient privacy, transparency, and fairness.

She implemented a strict code of ethics, ensuring that the company's products were developed with the highest moral standards in mind. Sarah's commitment to ethics not only helped the company build trust with clients but also attracted employees who shared the same values.

Practical Step:

Sarah worked closely with the legal and compliance teams to develop clear ethical guidelines. She emphasized the importance of these values in all company communications and actions, from product development to customer relations.

Conclusion

Through Sarah's leadership, InnovateTech successfully transformed from a struggling startup into a thriving market leader. Her ability to blend visionary thinking with decisive action, resilience, emotional intelligence, strategic agility, clear communication, and a commitment to integrity made her an exceptional CEO. By embodying these seven qualities, Sarah didn't just lead her company to success; she built a sustainable culture that would continue to thrive in the years to come.

For aspiring CEOs, Sarah's journey serves as a powerful example that these qualities are not just theoretical—they are practical and actionable. By adopting and refining these traits, any leader can elevate their organization to new heights.

3

The Power of CEO Resilience

Resilience is the unsung hero of successful leadership. In the business world, challenges are inevitable. Markets fluctuate, competitors rise, and sometimes even the best-laid plans fall apart. It's in these moments—when the odds are stacked against you—that the true power of resilience shows up.

Resilience isn't just about bouncing back from failure. It's about building the mental toughness to face setbacks with determination, learning from mistakes, and emerging stronger. As a CEO, your ability to stay strong in the face of adversity can determine your company's future. In this chapter, we'll dive into the importance of resilience, why it's essential for top leaders, and how you can cultivate it in your own leadership journey.

What Is Resilience?

At its core, resilience is the capacity to recover quickly from difficulties. It's about being able to adapt to change, cope with stress, and continue moving forward despite obstacles. But it's not just about surviving—it's about thriving after setbacks. Resilient CEOs don't just get through tough times; they learn from them, grow from them, and use them as stepping stones toward greater success.

Resilience isn't something you're born with; it's a mindset you can develop. Like any muscle, the more you practice resilience, the stronger it becomes. It's the ability to stay focused on your long-term goals, even when short-term challenges seem overwhelming.

Why Resilience Is Crucial for a CEO

As a CEO, you are the face of your company, and your ability to remain resilient in the face of adversity is a model for everyone in your organization. When things go wrong, your team looks to you for guidance and strength. If you falter, doubt can spread throughout the company, making it harder for everyone to recover. But if you remain calm, focused, and optimistic, your team will mirror your resilience, and together, you will find a way forward.

Here are a few key reasons why resilience is essential for a successful CEO:

- **It Helps You Lead in Crisis:** Every business faces crises—whether it's a financial downturn, a product failure, or a leadership change. How you respond in those critical moments will define the success of your company. Resilience allows you to navigate these crises with a level head and a clear plan.

- **It Builds Trust with Your Team:** A resilient CEO shows their team that no matter the challenge, they will face it together. By staying steady in tough times, you build trust and confidence within your organization.

- **It Encourages Innovation:** Resilience isn't just about bouncing back. It's also about learning from your mistakes and pushing forward with new ideas. Resilient CEOs are not afraid to experiment, fail, and try again, which often leads to the breakthroughs that keep their companies ahead of the curve.

The Resilient CEO Mindset

The most resilient CEOs share a few key traits. These aren't innate qualities; they're mindsets and habits that can be cultivated over time. Let's look at what makes up the resilient CEO mindset:

- **Embrace Failure as a Learning Opportunity:** Every successful CEO has experienced failure. The difference is how they respond to it. Resilient CEOs don't take failure personally—they view it as a lesson. They ask themselves, *What went wrong? What can I learn from this?* Instead of staying stuck in disappointment, they quickly shift focus to solutions and improvement.

- **Maintain a Positive Outlook:** Resilient CEOs are naturally optimistic. They understand that setbacks are temporary, and their vision for the company is strong enough to overcome any obstacle. A positive attitude helps them maintain perspective, stay motivated, and inspire their teams even during tough times.

- **Adaptability is Key:** The business world changes constantly. A resilient CEO knows that to survive, they must be flexible and willing to adapt. When things don't go as planned, they pivot, rework their strategies, and find new solutions. Instead of resisting change, they lean into it.

- **Emotional Control:** In high-stress situations, resilient CEOs stay calm and composed. They don't let fear, anger, or frustration cloud their judgment. Instead, they maintain emotional control, which allows them to make thoughtful, clear-headed decisions.

Practical Steps to Cultivate Resilience

Resilience is not something you can achieve overnight, but with intentional practice, you can build it into your leadership style. Here are some practical steps you can take to develop resilience:

1. Shift Your Perspective on Failure

Start viewing failure as feedback, not a setback. Ask yourself: *What can I learn from this experience?* Instead of dwelling on the disappointment, focus on how you can use the experience to improve your future decisions. This mindset shift helps you bounce back faster and become a stronger leader.

2. Build a Support System

Resilience is not about doing everything alone. Surround yourself with a network of mentors, peers, and advisors who can provide guidance when times get tough. Having a strong support system allows you to stay grounded and gain valuable perspectives during challenges.

3. Practice Stress-Relief Techniques

Stress is a natural part of being a CEO, but how you manage it will determine your ability to stay resilient. Practice techniques like meditation, exercise, or mindfulness to help manage stress and maintain mental clarity. Taking care of your physical and emotional well-being allows you to lead with strength.

4. Set Realistic, Long-Term Goals

One of the reasons many CEOs get overwhelmed is that they focus too much on short-term challenges. By setting long-term goals, you create a sense of purpose and direction. This gives you something to stay focused on when obstacles arise. Knowing that your efforts are building toward a bigger vision helps you stay resilient in the face of setbacks.

5. Celebrate Small Wins

Resilience isn't just about overcoming huge challenges—it's also about recognizing the small victories along the way. Every time you overcome a challenge, no matter how small, celebrate it. This helps reinforce the belief that you can get through tough times, one step at a time.

A Real-World Example of Resilience: The Story of Jack Thompson

Let's look at a real-world example of resilience in action. Jack Thompson is the CEO of a tech startup called InnovateX, which develops cutting-edge software solutions for small businesses. After two years of steady growth, the company faced a major setback: a competitor released a similar product, and a critical software bug caused a major delay in their product's launch. Sales dropped, customers became frustrated, and the company's reputation was on the line.

In the face of this crisis, Jack's resilience was put to the test. Instead of panicking or blaming his team, he focused on finding solutions. He held a company-wide meeting to be transparent about the challenges, assuring his team that they would work through it together. He acknowledged the mistake with the software bug and quickly assembled a task force to fix the issue.

Jack didn't let the failure define him. He and his team worked around the clock to fix the bug, communicate with customers, and reposition InnovateX's product to highlight its unique features. Within months, the company not only regained its customer base but also launched a new version of the product that outperformed the competition.

Jack's ability to stay calm, keep a positive outlook, and adapt to the situation was the key to the company's recovery. His resilience inspired his team to stay focused, and together, they emerged stronger than before.

Conclusion: Resilience—The Key to Long-Term Success

Resilience is not just about surviving tough times; it's about thriving in the face of adversity. As a CEO, your ability to stay resilient through challenges—big or small—can make the difference between success and failure. By cultivating a resilient mindset, embracing failure as a learning opportunity, and taking practical steps to build your emotional strength, you can lead your company through any storm.

Remember, the path to success is rarely a straight line. There will be bumps along the way. But with resilience, you will not only navigate those bumps—you will turn them into opportunities for growth, innovation, and success. Keep pushing forward, stay adaptable, and lead with resilience.

Practical Steps to Build CEO Confidence

Here are five practical steps you can take to build and nurture your confidence as a CEO:

1. Know Your Strengths and Weaknesses

Confidence starts with self-awareness. As a CEO, it's important to know what you excel at and where you might need support. By understanding your strengths, you can leverage them to lead with assurance. Conversely, knowing your weaknesses allows you to either improve them or surround yourself with a team that complements your skills.

Practical Tip:

Conduct a self-assessment to identify your strengths and areas for growth. Seek feedback from mentors, peers, and your team to gain a clear, honest perspective on your leadership qualities. Once you know where you excel, focus on amplifying those areas.

2. Take Action, Even When You're Uncertain

Confidence is built through action. The more you act, the more you learn, and the more confident you'll become. If you wait for the perfect moment or for all the pieces to fall into place, you may never take the leap. CEOs who hesitate or procrastinate end up missing opportunities.

Practical Tip:

Start small but take action. Make decisions without waiting for every piece of information. Trust that even if you make mistakes, you'll learn and adjust quickly. Over time, taking action will feel less intimidating and more natural.

3. Build a Support Network

Confidence is not just an individual trait—it's supported by those around you. Surround yourself with a trusted group of advisors, mentors, and peers who can offer guidance, feedback, and encouragement. Their support will help you feel more secure in your decisions and help you navigate difficult situations.

Practical Tip:

Identify mentors who have been through the challenges you're facing and can offer valuable advice. Create a network of peers—other CEOs or leaders who understand the pressures you face. Having people to turn to for perspective and advice builds confidence in your ability to lead.

4. Celebrate Small Wins

Confidence grows when you acknowledge your achievements, no matter how small. As a CEO, it's easy to get caught up in the pressures and challenges of running a business. But recognizing and celebrating your wins, as well as your team's accomplishments, can significantly boost your confidence.

Practical Tip:

Keep a "win journal" where you write down even the small successes. Whether it's a successful negotiation, a key hire, or solving a major problem, note your achievements and take time to appreciate your progress. Reflecting on your successes helps you realize that you are capable of leading your company.

5. Master Public Speaking and Communication

A key aspect of CEO confidence is the ability to speak with clarity and authority. Whether addressing the board, investors, or your team, your ability to communicate effectively influences how people perceive you. Improving your public speaking skills will help you feel more confident in these situations.

Practical Tip:

Practice your speaking skills in front of a mirror, record yourself, or participate in public speaking workshops. The more you practice, the more comfortable you'll become with speaking clearly and confidently in front of others.

Case Study: Confidence in Action - Sarah Kline, CEO of InnovateTech

Let's take a look at how confidence can make a real difference in a CEO's success through the story of Sarah Kline, the CEO of InnovateTech, a company that designs AI-driven solutions for healthcare.

Sarah took over as CEO of InnovateTech during a period of uncertainty. The company had recently faced a series of setbacks: a product launch failure, investor doubts, and a wave of employee turnover. Morale was low, and there were questions about the company's future. In the face of these challenges, Sarah had to quickly demonstrate her confidence, both to her team and to external stakeholders, in order to restore trust and move the company forward.

1. Stepping Up in the Face of Crisis

When Sarah first became CEO, she inherited a difficult situation. The previous CEO had stepped down, and there was a lot of uncertainty about the company's direction. Sarah had only been with the company for a few months before taking over, so many of the employees were skeptical of her leadership.

Instead of shying away from the responsibility, Sarah immediately set up an all-company meeting. In this meeting, she communicated her vision for InnovateTech's future, reassuring employees that the company had great potential. She spoke with such clarity and conviction that even the most skeptical employees began to believe in her vision.

2. Making Bold Decisions

As she settled into her role, Sarah faced another major challenge: the company's main product was failing in the market. The sales were below expectations, and the feedback from customers was harsh. There were calls from some executives to scale back operations and minimize risks. However, Sarah's confidence in the product and her belief in the team's ability to fix the issues led her to make a bold decision: instead of scaling back, InnovateTech would double down on improving the product and investing in a customer-centric redesign.

This decision was risky, but Sarah communicated it confidently, emphasizing the long-term vision and her trust in the team's ability to turn things around. She made sure to provide the resources the team needed to succeed and empowered them to take ownership of the changes. Her confidence in the product—and in her team—helped to restore faith in the company's direction.

3. Turning Around the Company

Over the next year, InnovateTech went through a complete transformation. The redesign of the product, driven by customer feedback, led to improved functionality and usability. Sarah's confident leadership inspired her team to work harder and smarter, and their renewed energy translated into success. Not only did sales improve, but the company also attracted new investors, which helped fund future growth.

Sarah's ability to project confidence, even in the face of significant challenges, helped turn InnovateTech into a thriving, innovative company once again.

Conclusion: Confidence Is the Foundation of Great Leadership

Confidence is more than just a trait—it's a skill that can be built, honed, and practiced. As a CEO, your confidence directly impacts your decision-making, your team's morale, and your ability to lead effectively. By knowing your strengths, taking action, building a support network, celebrating small wins, and mastering communication, you can build the confidence needed to lead your company to success.

Remember, confidence isn't about being perfect. It's about trusting in your ability to navigate challenges, inspire your team, and drive your company forward. The more you practice these principles, the more natural confidence will become, and the more powerful your leadership will be.

4

Humility in Leadership

Humility might not be the first quality that comes to mind when you think of powerful leaders. Often, we associate leadership with confidence, decisiveness, and strength. But the truth is, humility is an often-overlooked trait that can transform you into a more effective, relatable, and respected CEO.

Humility isn't about downplaying your achievements or pretending to be something you're not. It's about having a deep awareness of your own strengths and weaknesses, listening to others, and being open to feedback. A humble CEO fosters a culture of collaboration, encourages innovation, and builds a strong, loyal team. In this chapter, we'll explore the importance of humility in leadership and how you can cultivate this powerful trait to become a more effective CEO.

Why Humility Is Crucial for a Successful CEO

As a CEO, your leadership sets the tone for the entire company. Humility enables you to lead with empathy, build trust, and empower your team to reach their full potential. It creates an environment where employees feel valued and heard, which fosters loyalty and motivation. Here's why humility matters:

1. **Creates a Culture of Trust and Openness:** Humility allows you to be approachable and accessible. When employees see you as someone who values their input and ideas, they're more likely to be open, honest, and engaged in their work. A culture of trust and openness drives innovation and collaboration—two essential elements for growth.

2. **Builds Stronger Relationships:** Humble leaders prioritize relationships over ego. By recognizing that you don't have all the answers and that others can contribute valuable insights, you create an environment where your team feels respected and empowered to share their expertise.

3. **Encourages Personal and Organizational Growth:** Humility allows you to accept feedback—both positive and constructive. As a CEO, you need to be willing to listen to others' perspectives, admit when you're wrong, and make changes based on what you learn. This growth mindset helps both you and your organization evolve.

4. **Fosters Innovation:** When you lead with humility, you encourage creativity. Humble leaders are less focused on protecting their own ideas and more open to listening to others, which can result in innovative solutions and new ways of thinking.

5. **Demonstrates Self-Awareness:** Humility is rooted in self-awareness. As a CEO, this means recognizing that leadership is a continuous learning process. Humble CEOs understand that they are not infallible, and they are always seeking ways to improve themselves and their organizations.

The Benefits of Humility for a CEO

The impact of humility on your leadership style can be profound. Humility allows you to:

- **Inspire loyalty and trust** in your team by being authentic, transparent, and willing to listen.

- **Create a collaborative environment** where people feel comfortable offering ideas, taking risks, and working together to solve problems.

- **Facilitate growth**—both in yourself and in your company. Humility helps you recognize areas where you can improve and encourages the same mindset in your team.

- **Navigate challenges more effectively** by seeking out diverse perspectives and being open to feedback that can lead to better solutions.

A humble CEO doesn't need to have all the answers. What they need is the confidence to ask the right questions, listen deeply, and create an environment where others can thrive.

Practical Steps to Build Humility as a CEO

Humility may seem like a soft skill, but it's one of the most powerful traits a CEO can develop. Fortunately, humility is something you can actively cultivate and practice. Here are some practical steps you can take to build humility as a core leadership quality:

1. Lead by Example

As a CEO, your actions speak louder than words. If you want your team to adopt a culture of humility, you need to lead by example. This means being open about your own shortcomings, admitting when you don't have the answers, and acknowledging the contributions of others.

Practical Tip: Share your failures and lessons learned with your team. Acknowledge the people who helped you solve problems, and give credit where credit is due. When your team sees you practicing humility, they'll be more likely to do the same.

2. Be Open to Feedback

One of the most powerful ways to practice humility is to actively seek and embrace feedback—whether it's from your employees, mentors, or peers. A humble CEO understands that no matter how experienced or successful they are, there's always room for improvement.

Practical Tip:

Regularly ask for feedback from your team on your leadership style, decisions, and communication. Hold "feedback sessions" where employees feel comfortable offering constructive criticism. Be open-minded when receiving feedback and show gratitude for the insights you gain.

3. Acknowledge Your Team's Contributions

Humility means recognizing that your success is built on the efforts of others. A humble CEO is quick to credit their team for achievements, giving praise where it's deserved and making sure everyone feels valued.

Practical Tip: Publicly acknowledge your team's hard work, whether in meetings, emails, or company-wide communications. Regularly highlight the accomplishments of individuals or teams that contribute to the company's success. Celebrate collective wins, not just individual ones.

4. Stay Curious and Open to Learning

Humility involves a commitment to continuous learning. As a CEO, it's important to stay curious and open to new ideas, even if they challenge your current way of thinking. Humble leaders are lifelong learners, constantly seeking new knowledge and skills.

Practical Tip:

Take time to read books, attend seminars, and engage in discussions that challenge your thinking. Surround yourself with people who offer different perspectives, and be open to learning from them. Don't let your position as CEO close your mind to new possibilities.

5. Practice Active Listening

Humility is closely tied to the ability to listen—to truly hear what others are saying without jumping to conclusions or making judgments. When you listen actively, you make people feel respected and valued, and you gain insights that can improve your decisions.

Case Study: Humility in Action – Doug McMillon, CEO of Walmart

Doug McMillon, the CEO of Walmart, is a great example of how humility can shape effective leadership. When McMillon became CEO in 2014, Walmart was facing numerous challenges: increased competition from online retailers like Amazon, declining foot traffic to brick-and-mortar stores, and questions about the company's relevance in a rapidly changing retail environment.

Rather than coming in with an "I know best" mentality, McMillon demonstrated humility by first listening to employees, customers, and industry experts. He spent time visiting Walmart stores, talking to workers on the front lines, and gathering feedback from customers. He recognized that for Walmart to survive and thrive, it needed to adapt to the digital age and focus on improving the customer experience.

One of McMillon's key initiatives was to invest heavily in e-commerce and improve the company's technology infrastructure. However, he didn't take full credit for the success of these moves. He consistently acknowledged the contributions of Walmart's employees, including the technology teams, customer service staff, and store associates who played a role in the transformation.

Humility in Action:

McMillon's humility extended to how he handled the company's challenges. In 2015, when Walmart faced a significant slowdown in U.S. sales, McMillon didn't shy away from admitting that the company had made mistakes and was falling behind its competitors. Instead of becoming defensive, he focused on how the company could fix its problems and move forward. His openness about the challenges they were facing helped build trust and morale among employees, investors, and customers.

McMillon's approach of being humble, listening actively, and acknowledging the contributions of others helped Walmart become more nimble and forward-thinking. His leadership inspired a culture of collaboration within the company, which enabled Walmart to stay competitive in the digital age and continue to thrive.

Conclusion: Humility—The Quiet Strength of Great Leadership

Humility may seem like an understated quality, but it's a fundamental trait of great leadership. As a CEO, humility allows you to build trust, foster collaboration, and inspire loyalty. It creates a culture where employees feel respected and valued, and where innovation thrives.

By leading with humility, you not only become a more effective leader but also create an organization that is more adaptable, resilient, and capable of overcoming challenges. Remember, being humble doesn't mean downplaying your strengths; it means recognizing that your success is a team effort and that there is always room to learn and grow.

As you build your leadership style, make humility a cornerstone of your approach. Embrace feedback, acknowledge the contributions of others, and remain open to learning. With humility, you'll not only become a more successful CEO—you'll become a leader who truly makes a lasting impact.

5

Mastering Time Management

As a CEO, you are the captain of the ship, navigating through turbulent waters and steering your company toward its goals. However, one of the most crucial tools you have at your disposal isn't a high-powered strategy or a visionary business model—it's your time. Time management, when mastered, can be the difference between leading your company to success or feeling overwhelmed by the sheer volume of demands on your schedule.

Effective time management isn't just about working harder or longer hours; it's about working smarter. It's about understanding your priorities, setting boundaries, and aligning your time with what truly matters to your business and personal life. In this chapter, we will explore the essential time management skills every CEO needs and offer practical steps you can take to improve your own time management. We will also look at a real-life case study to show time management in action.

Why Time Management Is Critical for a CEO

Time is the one resource that every CEO, regardless of their industry, is equally constrained by. There are only 24 hours in a day, and as a CEO, you're likely juggling numerous responsibilities: overseeing day-to-day operations, setting strategic direction, engaging with investors, meeting with partners, and managing your team. Poor time management can lead to missed opportunities, burnout, and a lack of focus, while mastering time management allows you to allocate energy to high-priority tasks and lead with clarity.

Effective time management allows a CEO to:

- **Focus on What Matters Most**: By managing time effectively, you can prioritize tasks that have the greatest impact on your company's growth and your leadership role.

- **Maintain Strategic Vision**: A CEO needs to dedicate time for long-term planning, innovation, and company strategy. Without proper time management, it's easy to get bogged down in the daily grind.

- **Increase Productivity**: Time management techniques help you make the most of your workday, boosting both your efficiency and the productivity of those around you.

- **Reduce Stress and Burnout**: Properly allocating your time ensures that you aren't overcommitted. It helps you balance work and life, reducing stress and allowing for better decision-making.

At the heart of time management is understanding the value of your time and intentionally deciding how to use it. As a CEO, your time is a finite resource, and how you spend it will shape your company's future.

Practical Steps to Build Effective Time Management Skills

While mastering time management takes practice, there are a number of practical steps you can take to get started and significantly improve how you use your time. Here are some key strategies to implement in your daily routine:

1. Prioritize Your Tasks with the Eisenhower Matrix

The Eisenhower Matrix is a powerful tool for sorting tasks based on their urgency and importance. As a CEO, you need to consistently evaluate whether what you are working on is truly the best use of your time. The matrix divides tasks into four quadrants:

- **Quadrant 1 – Urgent and Important**: These are critical tasks that must be done immediately. Examples might include handling a crisis or making a key decision.

- **Quadrant 2 – Not Urgent but Important**: These tasks are essential for your long-term success but don't require immediate attention. Strategy meetings, innovation planning, and team development fall into this category.

- **Quadrant 3 – Urgent but Not Important**: These tasks feel urgent but aren't essential to your long-term goals. These are often distractions like some emails or certain meetings. Delegate these where possible.

- **Quadrant 4 – Not Urgent and Not Important**: These tasks are time-wasters—things like excessive social media browsing or unnecessary meetings. Minimize these activities.

Practical Tip:

At the beginning of each day or week, list your tasks and categorize them using the Eisenhower Matrix. This will help you focus on what truly matters and avoid getting bogged down in low-priority work.

2. Time Blocking

Time blocking is a technique where you allocate specific blocks of time in your calendar for different activities. By scheduling time for deep work, meetings, and even rest, you ensure that important tasks get the time they deserve and that distractions are minimized.

Practical Tip:

Each week, review your schedule and block out time for strategic thinking, meetings, and personal time. Include buffer time between tasks to allow for transitions. For example, block out "CEO Strategy Session" for an uninterrupted 2-hour block every Tuesday morning.

3. Delegate Effectively

As a CEO, you cannot—and should not—do everything yourself. One of the most important time management skills is knowing how to delegate effectively. By entrusting others with tasks, you can free up your time for high-level decision-making and leadership.

Practical Tip:

Identify tasks that can be delegated to other members of your team. For example, if you're spending too much time on operational tasks, delegate them to your COO or senior managers. Create a culture where your team understands that delegation is a sign of trust, not abdication.

4. Learn to Say No

As a CEO, it's easy to be pulled in multiple directions. However, saying "yes" to every opportunity or meeting can dilute your focus. Learning to say "no" to things that don't align with your strategic priorities is essential for effective time management.

Practical Tip:

Set clear criteria for what is worth your time. If an opportunity or meeting doesn't align with your top priorities, politely decline. Practice saying "no" with grace, such as: *"I appreciate the opportunity, but I'm currently focused on [insert priority]. Let's revisit this in a few months."*

5. Use Technology to Your Advantage

There are numerous tools and apps that can help you manage your time more efficiently. From task management apps to calendar systems, using technology can streamline your workflow and ensure you stay on track.

Practical Tip:

Use tools like Trello, Asana, or Monday.com to organize tasks and projects, and sync them with your calendar for easy tracking. Automate reminders for key deadlines, and use tools like Slack or Microsoft Teams to streamline communication and reduce unnecessary meetings.

Case Study: Time Management in Action – Indra Nooyi, Former CEO of PepsiCo

Indra Nooyi, the former CEO of PepsiCo, is a prime example of a leader who mastered time management to juggle the complexities of leading a global corporation. During her tenure at PepsiCo, Nooyi managed a company with over 250,000 employees and faced constant demands on her time from shareholders, employees, and customers. Yet, she was known for her disciplined approach to managing her schedule and staying focused on long-term strategy.

Strategic Time Blocking for High-Value Tasks

One of Nooyi's key time management techniques was strategic time blocking. She was known to schedule uninterrupted "thinking time" every day, where she would step away from meetings and immerse herself in high-level strategy. These blocks of time allowed her to focus on what truly mattered for PepsiCo's growth, whether it was evaluating new markets or refining the company's product offerings.

Delegation and Trust in Her Team

Nooyi also emphasized the importance of delegating effectively. She entrusted key decisions to her senior leadership team, allowing her to focus on the bigger picture. She recognized that being a CEO was about setting direction, making high-level decisions, and empowering others to execute on the details.

For example, instead of micromanaging operations, Nooyi relied on her senior executives to handle day-to-day issues while she focused on high-impact decisions like acquisitions and long-term growth strategies. She believed that giving her team autonomy led to greater innovation and allowed her to focus on areas where her leadership could make the most difference.

Saying No to Maintain Focus

Nooyi also mastered the art of saying "no." As PepsiCo grew, so did the number of opportunities, requests, and demands on her time. She was selective about what she engaged with, ensuring that her energy and focus were directed toward initiatives that aligned with PepsiCo's strategic goals.

For instance, when invited to sit on too many boards or take part in non-essential meetings, she would politely decline. She understood the value of her time and knew that being a CEO required making tough choices about how to allocate it.

Conclusion: Time Management – A CEOs Effectiveness

Effective time management is not just a skill—it's a mindset that enables you to focus on what's truly important and create lasting impact. As a CEO, your time is your most valuable resource, and how you manage it will determine your success. By prioritizing tasks, blocking time for critical activities, delegating, and setting clear boundaries, you can ensure that your time is spent on what moves the needle for your business.

The ability to manage your time effectively is a cornerstone of great leadership. If you want to excel as a CEO, start by taking control of your time. With the right practices in place, you can lead with clarity, drive innovation, and ultimately, guide your company toward its greatest successes.

6

Embracing Change

Change is the only constant in the business world. New technologies, shifting customer expectations, economic disruptions, and global challenges constantly reshape industries. For CEOs, the ability to embrace and manage change isn't just a necessity—it's a strategic advantage. Leaders who view change as an opportunity rather than a threat are the ones who thrive and lead their companies through transformation with confidence and success.

In this chapter, we'll explore why embracing change is essential for a CEO, how you can develop your change management skills, and the practical steps you can take to guide your company through periods of transition. We'll also dive into a real-life case study to see how one successful CEO turned change into an opportunity.

Why Embracing Change Is Crucial for a CEO

As a CEO, you're the one who sets the tone for your company's approach to change. The world doesn't wait for businesses to get comfortable, and staying stuck in outdated ways can quickly lead to irrelevance. But CEOs who embrace change with agility and vision can steer their companies through uncertainty and capitalize on new opportunities. Here's why embracing change is so important:

1. **Innovation and Competitive Advantage**: In a rapidly evolving market, businesses that don't change risk falling behind. A CEO who embraces change is always on the lookout for new innovations, whether it's through new technologies, improved processes, or expanded product lines.

2. **Resilience in Times of Crisis**: Change is often triggered by crises. A CEO who is comfortable with change can pivot quickly in response to unexpected challenges—whether it's a global pandemic, economic downturn, or industry disruption. This resilience helps ensure long-term business survival.

3. **Attracting and Retaining Talent**: Modern employees are attracted to companies that embrace innovation and growth. A culture that fosters continuous change is more likely to attract top talent who want to be part of an evolving, dynamic environment.

4. **Long-Term Success**: Business leaders who can navigate change effectively build companies that are adaptable and sustainable. These leaders are focused on the future, looking at how the company can evolve and stay relevant in a world that never stops changing.

Practical Steps to Develop Change Management Skills

As a CEO, you must be equipped not only to handle change but also to lead your company through it. Effective change management requires a clear vision, strong communication, and the ability to align your team with new goals. Here are some practical steps you can take to improve your change management skills and lead your organization through successful transformations:

1. Cultivate a Growth Mindset

A growth mindset—the belief that abilities and intelligence can be developed through hard work, dedication, and learning—is a critical foundation for embracing change. As a CEO, you must view challenges and changes as opportunities to learn, grow, and improve. This mindset will help you and your team approach new initiatives with enthusiasm rather than resistance.

Practical Tip:

Start every day with a learning attitude. Seek out new information, whether it's through reading industry reports, listening to podcasts, or attending seminars. Encourage your team to continuously improve and embrace new ideas by fostering a culture of innovation and curiosity.

2. Lead with Vision and Clarity

When change is necessary, people often feel uncertain and anxious. As the CEO, it's your job to provide clarity and direction. Articulate a clear vision of where the company is going and why the change is happening. Paint a picture of the future that excites and motivates your team.

Practical Tip:

Before rolling out any major change, take the time to communicate the purpose behind it. Share the vision of how this change will positively impact the company and its people. Provide concrete examples of how the new direction will benefit both the company and individual employees.

3. Involve Your Team Early and Often

The more people feel included in the change process, the less resistance you'll face. Involve key stakeholders early in the planning stages and continuously engage them throughout the implementation process. Listen to their concerns, incorporate their feedback, and address any questions they may have.

Practical Tip:

Create a communication plan that includes regular updates and opportunities for feedback. Hold town hall meetings, send email newsletters, or host smaller focus groups to gather input and ensure transparency. Keep the conversation open and honest.

4. Be Flexible and Adaptive

Change is rarely a smooth, linear process. There will be setbacks and unforeseen obstacles. A successful CEO remains flexible and adaptive during the transition, pivoting when necessary while maintaining focus on the end goal. Embrace agility by encouraging your team to stay open-minded and adaptable.

5. Build a Strong Change Management Team

While you're ultimately the leader, you can't manage change alone. Assemble a team of key leaders within your organization who are aligned with the vision and can help implement the change. These individuals will be your change champions, driving the transformation and helping others navigate the shift.

6. Communicate Transparently and Frequently

Communication is perhaps the most vital element of managing change. Whether the change is big or small, consistent, honest, and clear communication will build trust and minimize confusion. Be transparent about the reasons for the change and the expected outcomes.

Case Study: Howard Schultz – Transforming Starbucks Through Change

Howard Schultz, the former CEO of Starbucks, provides an excellent example of how effective change management can lead to significant organizational growth. Schultz joined Starbucks in 1982 and, by 1987, had purchased the company from its original owners and began to reshape it into a global coffee empire.

However, it wasn't always smooth sailing. By the mid-2000s, Starbucks faced a slowdown in growth, rising competition, and a decline in the customer experience that had once made the brand so successful. Schultz realized that Starbucks needed to undergo a massive transformation if it was going to survive the rapidly changing retail environment.

Embracing Change with Vision and Clarity

Schultz made the bold decision to close 900 underperforming stores and overhaul the Starbucks experience. He embraced technology, including the introduction of the Starbucks mobile app, which allowed customers to order ahead and streamline the experience. He also refocused on quality, closing stores for several days to retrain employees on the brand's core values and customer service standards.

At the heart of Schultz's strategy was a clear vision: to return Starbucks to its roots as a "third place" where customers could feel at home. He communicated this vision clearly to employees, customers, and investors. Schultz also introduced the concept of "lean thinking" into the company, streamlining operations and removing unnecessary complexities.

Involving the Team and Leading with Empathy

Schultz's leadership was characterized by empathy and inclusivity. He personally communicated the company's changes to employees, reassuring them that the brand was being reinvigorated for their benefit. His emotional intelligence shone through as he made decisions based not only on profitability but also on the welfare of Starbucks employees, offering health insurance and stock options even for part-time workers.

Schultz's decision to focus on people—both employees and customers—during a time of significant change allowed Starbucks to not only survive but thrive in a competitive industry.

Adapting to Setbacks and Leading Through Crisis

Starbucks didn't immediately recover, and Schultz faced harsh criticism from both Wall Street and the media. However, he remained adaptable and open to learning from the challenges. For instance, the initial rollout of the mobile app wasn't as smooth as expected, but Schultz quickly adjusted the strategy, working with the tech team to improve functionality and customer experience.

In 2008, when the global financial crisis hit, Schultz didn't retreat from change—he leaned into it. He understood that, in times of economic uncertainty, customers' behaviors would shift. Rather than focusing solely on expansion, Schultz doubled down on improving the customer experience, adding new, innovative products like the Starbucks Reserve line and premium coffee offerings.

The Results

Under Schultz's leadership, Starbucks rebounded, more than tripling its global store count and re-establishing its position as a leader in the coffee industry. Schultz's ability to embrace change, communicate effectively, and adapt to challenges was key to Starbucks' remarkable transformation.

Conclusion: Change Is an Opportunity, Not a Threat

As a CEO, the ability to embrace and manage change is one of the most important skills you can develop. Change will always be a part of business life, and how you handle it will determine your company's future success. By cultivating a growth mindset, leading with vision, involving your team, and staying flexible, you can turn periods of transition into opportunities for growth, innovation, and competitive advantage.

Remember, the most successful CEOs are those who don't just survive change— they thrive in it. By mastering change management, you position yourself and your company to not only navigate disruptions but to lead the way forward.

7

Executive Financial Literacy

As the CEO of a company, you're not just responsible for its growth, culture, and strategy—you are also the steward of its financial health. The decisions you make today will impact your company's bottom line for years to come, and understanding the language of finance is critical to those decisions. Whether you're raising capital, planning for growth, or managing profitability, financial literacy and financial modelling are the tools you need to navigate the complexities of business.

In this chapter, we'll break down the key concepts of financial literacy and financial modelling, and offer practical steps to help you build your financial management skills. Finally, we'll explore a real-life case study to show how one CEO's strong financial acumen led to remarkable business success.

Why Financial Literacy is Essential for a CEO

Financial literacy isn't just for CFOs or accountants—it's a critical skill for every CEO. A deep understanding of your company's finances allows you to make data-driven decisions, allocate resources efficiently, and predict the financial outcomes of various business strategies.

As a CEO, your financial literacy empowers you to:

1. **Make Informed Decisions**: Whether you're deciding to enter a new market, launch a new product, or restructure your company, having a strong understanding of financial metrics helps you assess the potential risks and rewards.

2. **Communicate with Investors and Stakeholders**: Investors expect you to speak confidently about your company's financials. By mastering financial concepts, you can build trust with investors, raise capital more effectively, and ensure transparency.

3. **Guide Company Strategy**: Financial literacy allows you to align your strategic goals with realistic financial forecasts. When you understand key financial indicators, you can better direct your company's growth trajectory.

4. **Manage Cash Flow**: Cash flow is the lifeblood of your business. Understanding how to forecast and manage cash flow ensures that your business has enough liquidity to operate, grow, and weather difficult periods.

What is Financial Modelling?

Financial modelling is the process of creating a mathematical representation of your company's financial performance. This model is often used to forecast future financial performance, simulate different business scenarios, and make strategic decisions. Financial models can help you:

- **Forecast future revenue, expenses, and profits**

- **Assess the impact of potential investments or strategic decisions**

- **Evaluate the feasibility of business opportunities**

- **Understand your company's valuation for fundraising or exit purposes**

A solid financial model helps you translate business strategy into numbers, providing a roadmap for making more confident, data-driven decisions.

Practical Steps to Build Your Financial Management Skills

Financial literacy doesn't require you to become an expert accountant, but it does require you to be comfortable navigating financial statements, understanding key metrics, and making informed decisions based on financial data. Here are the key steps to building your financial acumen:

1. Understand the Core Financial Statements

As a CEO, you must be fluent in the three key financial statements: the income statement, the balance sheet, and the cash flow statement. These documents provide insights into your company's profitability, financial position, and cash flow.

- **Income Statement**: This shows your company's revenues, costs, and profits over a specific period of time (e.g., quarterly or annually). Understanding your income statement helps you assess whether your company is making money or losing it.

- **Balance Sheet**: This provides a snapshot of your company's assets, liabilities, and equity at a specific point in time. It helps you understand your company's financial health and the value of its assets versus its debts.

- **Cash Flow Statement**: This tracks the movement of cash in and out of your business. It helps you understand whether your company has enough liquidity to meet its obligations, make investments, and grow.

Practical Tip:

Schedule regular meetings with your CFO or financial team to review these statements. Get comfortable asking questions like: "What does this number mean?" or "How does this affect our bottom line?" Understanding the answers will build your confidence in financial matters.

2. Learn Key Financial Metrics

Understanding key financial metrics is crucial for evaluating your company's performance and making decisions. Some of the most important metrics include:

- **Gross Profit Margin**: This shows how efficiently your company is producing goods or services. A high margin indicates good profitability.

- **Operating Profit Margin (EBIT)**: This shows how efficiently your business operates before interest and taxes are factored in.

- **Net Profit Margin**: This is the final measure of profitability, showing how much profit you make after all expenses, taxes, and costs.

- **Return on Assets (ROA)**: This shows how effectively your company is using its assets to generate profit.

- **Current Ratio**: This measures your company's ability to cover short-term liabilities with short-term assets, which is critical for managing liquidity.

Practical Tip:

Focus on learning just a few key metrics at first, then gradually expand your knowledge. Track these metrics regularly and ask your financial team to explain trends and anomalies.

3. Build a Simple Financial Model

You don't need to be a financial expert to build a basic financial model. A simple financial model can help you forecast future revenues, expenses, and profits based on different assumptions (like sales growth or cost changes). Here's how to build a simple model:

- **Step 1: Gather Data**: Start with historical financial data—your past income statements and balance sheets. This will form the foundation of your model.

- **Step 2: Define Assumptions**: What assumptions will drive your model? For example, you might assume a 10% increase in sales or a 5% rise in production costs over the next year.

- **Step 3: Create Revenue Projections**: Use historical data to project future revenues. For example, if your sales grew by 15% last year, you might assume a similar growth rate.

- **Step 4: Estimate Expenses**: Look at your fixed and variable expenses, then forecast them based on the assumptions you've made. Factor in things like rent, salaries, and material costs.

- **Step 5: Analyze the Results**: Once you've built the model, analyze the results. Do you have enough cash flow to cover your expenses? Are you hitting your profit targets?

Practical Tip:

Start simple—use Excel or Google Sheets to build your first model. There are also online tools like LivePlan or QuickBooks that can help you build financial projections without needing to be an expert.

---

4. Learn to Use Scenario Planning

Scenario planning is a valuable tool for CEOs to understand the financial outcomes of different decisions or market conditions. For example, how would a 20% drop in sales affect your company's bottom line? How would a significant increase in raw material costs impact your profitability?

Practical Tip:

Create multiple scenarios in your financial model (e.g., "Best Case," "Most Likely Case," and "Worst Case"). Use these models to guide strategic decisions and to prepare for uncertainty.

---

5. Seek Financial Advice and Mentorship

As a CEO, it's important to have a network of trusted advisors who can help you navigate complex financial decisions. This might include your CFO, financial consultants, or mentors with deep financial expertise.

Practical Tip:

Surround yourself with people who have a strong financial background and don't be afraid to ask for advice. A mentor or advisor can help you see things from a different perspective and challenge your assumptions.

Case Study: Jeff Bezos and Amazon's Financial Acumen

One of the most compelling examples of a CEO using financial literacy and modelling to drive success is Jeff Bezos, the founder and former CEO of Amazon. Bezos is widely recognized for his ability to make bold, data-driven decisions that were grounded in solid financial analysis. Early on in Amazon's journey, Bezos used financial modelling to assess the long-term viability of his business model, even when investors were skeptical.

Financial Modelling to Guide Expansion

In Amazon's early years, Bezos faced a tough decision: Should the company focus on immediate profitability or reinvest every dollar back into growing its infrastructure? Bezos recognized that Amazon's success depended on scaling quickly, which meant he needed to invest heavily in technology, warehouses, and logistics.

To forecast Amazon's long-term profitability, Bezos developed a financial model that included aggressive growth assumptions. His model projected that, while Amazon might operate at a loss in the short term, the company's investment in infrastructure would lead to enormous efficiencies and competitive advantages in the long run.

Building a Resilient Financial Strategy

Bezos also embraced scenario planning. He modelled how different factors—such as changes in consumer behavior, shipping costs, and global market expansion—would affect Amazon's finances. This allowed him to make bold decisions, such as entering international markets early on or investing heavily in Amazon Web Services (AWS), even when the company wasn't profitable.

Bezos's financial models didn't just guide Amazon's expansion—they also helped him communicate a clear vision to investors. He was able to explain his long-term strategy and provide financial data that reassured investors that Amazon was on the right path, even when it wasn't making immediate profits.

The Result

Today, Amazon is one of the most valuable companies in the world, with a market capitalization in the trillions of dollars. Bezos's ability to understand and apply financial literacy and modelling was instrumental in navigating Amazon's growth and positioning the company for long-term success.

Conclusion: Financial Literacy as a CEO's Superpower

Financial literacy and financial modelling are not optional skills for a modern CEO—they are essential. By understanding your company's financial statements, learning key metrics, and building simple models, you can make smarter, data-driven decisions that propel your company toward long-term success.

As demonstrated in the case of Jeff Bezos, strong financial acumen enables CEOs to navigate uncertainty, make bold investments

8

Leadership in Action

L eadership is the cornerstone of any successful organization, and as a CEO, the leadership decisions you make can define the future of your company. But leadership is not a one-size-fits-all approach. The best CEOs recognize that different situations require different leadership styles. Being able to assess the context, your team's needs, and your own strengths is crucial for leading effectively.

In this chapter, we'll dive into the various leadership styles, explore the characteristics of each, and discuss the importance of decisive leadership. We'll also provide practical steps to help you determine your leadership style and refine your skills. Finally, we'll look at a real-life case study to see leadership in action at the highest level.

Why Leadership Matters for a CEO

As a CEO, your leadership sets the tone for your entire organization. Your leadership will inspire the culture, drive strategic initiatives, and motivate your team to achieve the company's vision. But leadership is more than just a title; it's a set of behaviors and decisions that build trust, engagement, and performance.

Decisive leadership is especially important in today's fast-paced, often volatile business environment. Employees, investors, and stakeholders look to the CEO for direction, and how you lead can affect everything from company morale to the bottom line. Understanding the different leadership styles and how to apply them is a key part of navigating the complexities of running a business.

Leadership Styles: Understanding the Spectrum

There's no single way to lead a company—different circumstances and company cultures call for different leadership approaches. Below, we'll explore the four primary leadership styles and the characteristics of each. Most CEOs blend elements from several styles, but understanding where you naturally lean can help you become more self-aware and effective in your leadership.

1. The Transformational Leader

A transformational leader is someone who focuses on inspiring and motivating employees to innovate and create positive change. They lead by example, challenging the status quo and pushing for continual improvement and growth. Transformational leaders tend to be visionary and have a long-term perspective on organizational goals.

- **Characteristics**:
    - Strong communication skills, able to articulate a compelling vision
    - High energy, enthusiasm, and passion
    - Focus on innovation and continuous improvement
    - Emphasis on developing others and empowering the team

- **Best For**: Companies going through periods of significant change or those needing a shift in culture and mindset. Transformational leaders are often found in high-growth startups or industries experiencing disruption.

2. The Transactional Leader

Transactional leadership focuses on structure, order, and clear performance expectations. Transactional leaders reward employees for meeting goals and punish them for failing to meet performance standards. This leadership style works well in environments where routine tasks and established processes are key to business success.

- **Characteristics**:

    o Strong emphasis on structure, processes, and clear objectives

    o Rewards for meeting specific targets and penalties for failure

    o Focus on maintaining the status quo and operational efficiency

- **Best For**: Companies with well-defined processes, industries with heavy regulations, or businesses in a mature phase where stability is more important than change.

---

3. The Servant Leader

A servant leader focuses on the well-being of their team. They lead with humility, prioritize the needs of others, and focus on empowering their employees to reach their full potential. Servant leaders build strong relationships with their teams and are deeply committed to helping others succeed.

- **Characteristics**:

    o Empathy and emotional intelligence

    o Focus on mentoring and developing employees

    o Strong listening skills and a collaborative approach

    o Leading by serving others, not through authority

- **Best For**: Companies that emphasize strong internal culture, collaboration, and employee development. This style is particularly effective in industries like healthcare, education, and non-profits, where the focus is on service.

---

4. The Autocratic Leader

An autocratic leader makes decisions unilaterally, without seeking input from others. This leadership style is very directive and can be effective when quick, decisive action is needed. Autocratic leadership works best in crisis situations where fast, clear decisions are critical.

- **Characteristics**:

  o Clear, direct decision-making with minimal input from others

  o Strong control over processes and people

  o Quick decision-making during emergencies or high-pressure situations

  o Less emphasis on employee collaboration or empowerment

- **Best For**: Crisis management or highly structured environments like the military or manufacturing sectors, where speed and efficiency are critical.

5. The Democratic (Participative) Leader

A democratic leader encourages input from team members before making decisions. They value collaboration and collective problem-solving. This style fosters high levels of engagement and trust, as employees feel that their opinions are heard and valued.

- **Characteristics**:

  o Collaboration and active involvement of the team in decision-making

  o Open communication and shared responsibility

  o Focus on team consensus and collective problem-solving

- **Best For**: Creative industries, technology startups, or companies looking to foster innovation, where employee engagement and input can lead to better outcomes.

The Importance of Decisive Leadership

While each leadership style has its merits, a key characteristic of successful CEOs is decisiveness. As a CEO, you will face countless decisions—some small, some monumental—and your ability to make timely and informed decisions is critical to your success.

Decisiveness doesn't mean being rigid or inflexible. Rather, it means making decisions with confidence after gathering sufficient information, listening to advisors, and weighing your options. A decisive leader doesn't hesitate or second-guess themselves for too long, but also understands when to pivot if new information arises.

Decisiveness is important for several reasons:

1. **Builds Trust**: Teams trust leaders who make decisions and take responsibility for those decisions. If you constantly hesitate or show indecision, it can create uncertainty in your team.

2. **Ensures Momentum**: In fast-paced industries, delays in decision-making can cause a company to fall behind. A decisive CEO ensures that the company maintains momentum and stays on track.

3. **Drives Accountability**: Decisive leaders take ownership of their decisions, whether the outcomes are positive or negative. This fosters a culture of accountability within the organization.

Practical Steps to Determine and Develop Your Leadership Style

To be an effective CEO, you need to understand your natural leadership style and how to adapt it to different situations. Here are some practical steps to help you develop your leadership skills:

1. Self-Assessment

Start by reflecting on your natural tendencies. Do you lean toward empowering others (servant leadership)? Are you more focused on achieving results quickly (transactional or autocratic)? Or do you inspire change and innovation (transformational)? Taking an honest self-assessment can help you identify your strengths and areas for growth.

Practical Tip:

Use leadership assessments like the **Leadership Styles Inventory** or the **DiSC Personality Assessment** to gain insight into your preferred leadership style.

2. Seek Feedback

While self-assessments are valuable, feedback from your team, peers, and mentors is essential. Ask your employees how they perceive your leadership. Do they find you empowering, approachable, or decisive? Regular feedback helps you calibrate your leadership approach and adapt to different situations.

Practical Tip:

Set up regular one-on-one meetings with key team members to ask for honest feedback about your leadership style and how you can improve.

3. Adapt to the Situation

Great leaders know that the most effective style depends on the context. For example, during a crisis, you may need to adopt a more autocratic, decisive approach. During periods of growth or innovation, a transformational or democratic style may be more appropriate. The key is to assess the situation and adapt accordingly.

Practical Tip:

Practice flexibility by consciously shifting between leadership styles based on the situation. For example, in a brainstorming session, be more democratic; in a budget meeting, be more transactional.

4. Develop Emotional Intelligence

No matter your leadership style, emotional intelligence (EQ) is a vital skill. The ability to understand and manage your emotions, as well as recognize and influence the emotions of others, will help you lead with empathy, build stronger relationships, and navigate complex situations.

Practical Tip:

Work on developing your EQ by practicing active listening, managing stress, and cultivating empathy for your team.

---

5. Lead by Example

No matter your leadership style, one of the most effective ways to lead is by setting an example. If you want your team to be accountable, be accountable. If you want them to be innovative, show that you're willing to take risks and try new things. Leading by example builds credibility and trust.

Practical Tip:

Model the behaviors you want to see in your team. Whether it's a commitment to excellence, continuous learning, or collaboration, your actions should align with your words.

Case Study: Satya Nadella and Transforming Microsoft's Leadership

When Satya Nadella took over as CEO of Microsoft in 2014, the company was struggling. It had fallen behind in key areas like cloud computing, and its culture was seen as rigid and competitive rather than collaborative. Nadella understood that in order to succeed, he needed to transform Microsoft's culture and leadership style.

Leadership Transformation

Nadella adopted a **transformational leadership** approach, emphasizing empathy, collaboration, and growth mindset. He shifted Microsoft's focus from a "know-it-all" culture to a "learn-it-all" culture, encouraging employees to innovate and learn from failures. He also fostered open communication, transparency, and cross-departmental collaboration.

Decisive Leadership in Action

Nadella also demonstrated **decisive leadership** when he led Microsoft's pivot toward cloud computing. Despite the company's legacy in software and hardware, Nadella made the bold decision to invest heavily in Azure, Microsoft's cloud platform. This shift was a clear departure from the company's historical focus, but Nadella's decisiveness and confidence paid off, positioning Microsoft as a leader in the cloud space.

The Result

Under Nadella's leadership, Microsoft's stock price tripled, and the company's culture shifted from being competitive and siloed to being inclusive and innovative. His combination of transformational leadership, decisiveness, and focus on empathy and collaboration transformed Microsoft into a modern tech giant.

Conclusion: The Power of Leadership

As a CEO, your leadership style is one of the most powerful tools you have at your disposal. By understanding the different leadership styles, adapting to the needs of your organization, and developing key leadership qualities like emotional intelligence and decisiveness, you can guide your company to new heights.

Leadership isn't just about giving orders—it's about inspiring, motivating, and empowering your team to perform at their best. Whether you're a transformational, transactional, or servant leader, the most important thing is to lead with authenticity, clarity, and purpose.

9

Building High-Performance Teams

One of the most crucial tasks for any CEO is building and nurturing high-performance teams. A high-performing team can drive innovation, increase productivity, and maintain a competitive edge in the market. The success of your company depends not just on the strategic decisions you make, but on the teams you build to execute those decisions. As the CEO, your ability to create, develop, and lead these teams is fundamental to achieving operational excellence and long-term growth.

In this chapter, we will explore various methods CEOs use to build high-performance teams, highlight the most effective techniques, and provide practical steps you can take to improve your own team-building skills. We'll also dive into a real-life case study to demonstrate how a CEO successfully built a high-performance team that drove operational excellence.

The Importance of High-Performance Teams

High-performance teams are more than just groups of people working together. They are cohesive, motivated, and aligned with a common goal. They operate with high levels of trust, accountability, and collaboration. For a CEO, assembling and leading such a team is one of the most powerful levers to drive the organization forward.

A high-performance team can:

- **Deliver results consistently**: These teams are focused on achieving their goals and do so efficiently and effectively.

- **Adapt to change**: High-performance teams are agile and can pivot quickly in response to market changes or new opportunities.

- **Drive innovation**: When employees feel empowered and supported, they bring creative ideas that can disrupt industries and lead to breakthroughs.

- **Enhance company culture**: The collective mindset of a high-performance team sets the tone for the rest of the organization. A motivated, aligned team breeds a positive, productive work environment.

As the CEO, you are the architect of your organization's high-performance culture. But how do you build it?

Methods for Building High-Performance Teams

There are several methods that CEOs and executives use to build high-performance teams. Each method has its strengths and applications, but some are more universally effective than others. Below, we'll break down the most popular methods for team-building then explore which one is the most effective for creating a sustainable high-performance culture.

1. Hiring for Fit and Skill

One of the first steps in building a high-performance team is recruiting the right people. Hiring for fit ensures that the individuals align with your company's core values and culture. Hiring for skill ensures they have the necessary competencies to execute their roles.

- **What Works**: A solid hiring process that assesses both technical skills and cultural fit. A good balance between these two ensures you have employees who not only excel at their tasks but also mesh well with the team dynamics.

- **Challenges**: Sometimes, cultural fit can be overemphasized, leading to a homogeneous team that lacks diverse perspectives.

Tip:

Prioritize diversity in experience, thinking, and background to ensure your team has the variety needed to solve problems from different angles.

2. Clear Goals and Expectations

A team with clear, measurable goals is a team with a roadmap to success. Setting clear expectations and aligning your team around a shared vision gives them a sense of purpose and focus. When everyone understands the objective and their role in achieving it, they can work in harmony toward common goals.

- **What Works**: CEOs who use **OKRs (Objectives and Key Results)** or **SMART goals** (Specific, Measurable, Achievable, Relevant, Time-bound) to set objectives and track progress.

- **Challenges**: Without clear milestones, teams may lose sight of their purpose, leading to misaligned efforts and decreased productivity.

Tip:

Break down long-term goals into smaller, actionable tasks. Regularly revisit these goals and adjust them based on market shifts or team feedback.

3. Cultivating Trust and Psychological Safety

The best teams are built on trust. When team members trust each other, they are more likely to collaborate, share ideas, and take calculated risks. Creating an environment of psychological safety—where employees feel comfortable expressing their ideas without fear of judgment—can be a game-changer in building a high-performing team.

- **What Works**: Transparent communication and vulnerability. As a CEO, being open about challenges and acknowledging your own mistakes helps build trust across the organization.

- **Challenges**: Without trust, employees may withhold information, work in silos, or avoid giving feedback. This can stifle innovation and slow down decision-making.

4. Fostering Collaboration and Accountability

High-performing teams are collaborative but also hold each other accountable. Accountability ensures that everyone is responsible for their part in achieving the team's goals. However, collaboration and accountability must go hand in hand. Without collaboration, teams can become siloed and less efficient. Without accountability, team members might not fully commit to their responsibilities.

- **What Works**: Regular check-ins, paired with a collaborative culture, help ensure that everyone is on track and contributing to the team's success. Setting up cross-functional teams and encouraging knowledge-sharing helps teams leverage each other's strengths.

- **Challenges**: A lack of accountability can result in team members not pulling their weight, leading to frustration among others.

5. Investing in Continuous Learning and Development

High-performance teams thrive in environments where continuous improvement is the norm. Providing opportunities for professional development—whether through formal training, mentorship programs, or on-the-job learning—ensures that your team stays sharp and ready to take on new challenges.

- **What Works**: Leaders who provide access to learning resources, encourage team members to attend industry events, or create in-house training programs help foster a culture of growth and curiosity.

- **Challenges**: Companies that neglect employee development may find that their teams become stagnant, less innovative, and disengaged over time.

Tip:

Establish a mentorship program within the organization and allow employees to cross-train in different roles to develop new skills.

The Most Effective Method: A Holistic Approach

While all of the above methods are crucial, the most effective way to build a high-performance team is to integrate **all** of them into a cohesive strategy. The best CEOs don't just hire well or set clear goals—they actively foster an environment that combines clear expectations, trust, collaboration, and continuous learning.

The most successful CEOs build teams that are aligned in purpose, equipped with the right skills, held accountable, and continuously developing. By embedding a culture of trust, transparency, and mutual support, CEOs create environments where teams can thrive, innovate, and drive the company toward success.

Practical Steps to Develop Your High-Performance Team-Building Skills

Here are some actionable steps you can take to develop your ability to build high-performance teams:

1. **Evaluate Your Current Team's Strengths and Weaknesses**

   Start by assessing your team's current dynamics. Are there gaps in skills or trust? Are your goals clearly defined? Understanding these dynamics will help you take the right actions.

2. **Hire for Both Skills and Cultural Fit**

   When hiring, focus on candidates who not only have the skills to excel in their roles but who also align with your company's values. Build diversity in both thought and experience to enrich your team's capabilities.

3. **Set Clear, Measurable Goals**

   Use OKRs or SMART goals to define success clearly. Make sure everyone on your team knows exactly what's expected and how their role fits into the bigger picture.

4. **Create a Culture of Trust**

   Lead with transparency and encourage open communication. Ensure that feedback is both given and received regularly. Hold yourself accountable and admit when you don't have all the answers.

5. **Encourage Collaboration**

   Build a collaborative culture by promoting cross-functional work and team-building activities. Celebrate team wins and acknowledge individual contributions.

6. **Invest in Development**

   Provide regular opportunities for your team to learn and grow. Offer training, mentorship, and cross-functional projects to help employees expand their skill sets.

7. **Recognize and Reward Performance**

   Publicly acknowledge team successes and individual contributions. Recognizing effort and achievement boosts morale and reinforces a high-performance culture.

Case Study: Indra Nooyi and PepsiCo's High-Performance Team

Indra Nooyi, former CEO of PepsiCo, is a great example of a leader who built a high-performance team to drive operational excellence. When Nooyi took over as CEO in 2006, PepsiCo was facing significant challenges, including stagnant growth and a fragmented brand image. Her solution was to focus on creating a high-performance, purpose-driven culture that aligned with both financial goals and social responsibility.

Building the Right Team

Nooyi prioritized hiring top talent who could drive innovation while also aligning with PepsiCo's values of sustainability, diversity, and social impact. She also fostered an environment of transparency and collaboration, making sure that employees at all levels felt valued and heard. By focusing on hiring the right people and empowering them to take ownership, she was able to create a culture of high performance.

Decisive Leadership and Operational Excellence

Nooyi also demonstrated decisive leadership when she made bold moves, such as pushing for healthier product options in PepsiCo's portfolio and expanding the company's presence in emerging markets. These decisions were backed by strong teamwork, clear goals, and a commitment to long-term sustainability.

The Results

Under Nooyi's leadership, PepsiCo's revenue grew by more than 80%, and the company expanded into new product categories like healthier snacks and beverages. Her focus on building a high-performance team allowed PepsiCo to transform its culture, innovate its product offerings, and maintain operational excellence.

Conclusion: Building High-Performance Teams is a Strategic Priority for CEOs

As a CEO, building high-performance teams is not just a responsibility—it's a strategic imperative. The success of your organization depends on the people you bring together, how well they collaborate, and how they execute on the goals you set. By prioritizing trust, clear goals, collaboration, and continuous learning, you can create a high-performance culture that drives long-term growth and operational excellence.

High-performance teams don't just happen—they are created through deliberate action, strong leadership, and a commitment to fostering the right environment for success. As you continue your journey as a CEO, remember that your ability to build and lead these teams is one of your most powerful assets.

10

Developing Operational Excellence

Operational excellence is more than just a buzzword; it is a mindset and a set of practices that help a company consistently deliver superior performance, maintain a competitive edge, and achieve sustainable growth. For a CEO, fostering operational excellence means creating an environment where every process, every decision, and every action is focused on maximizing efficiency, reducing waste, and improving quality.

In this chapter, we will explore what operational excellence truly means, how CEOs can foster it within their organizations, and the various methods and strategies to achieve it. We will also dive into a real-life case study of how a CEO turned operational excellence into a core competitive advantage.

What is Operational Excellence?

At its core, operational excellence is about creating processes that consistently deliver high-quality results with the least amount of waste, cost, and effort. It's about **optimizing the entire value chain**—from production to customer service, and even back-office functions—to ensure your company operates at peak efficiency.

Operational excellence is not a one-time achievement; it's an ongoing commitment to continuous improvement. It's a cultural shift that requires leadership, engagement, and discipline from everyone in the company. It touches all aspects of business, from supply chain management and production processes to human resources and customer relations.

As a CEO, fostering operational excellence in your organization ensures that your business can **scale efficiently**, **adapt to change**, and consistently meet customer expectations. This becomes a significant driver for profitability, customer loyalty, and long-term success.

Methods Used by CEOs to Achieve Operational Excellence

Several methods and frameworks are used by CEOs to establish and sustain operational excellence. These frameworks help structure a company's efforts and ensure that improvements are made across every area of the business. Below are some of the most commonly used methods.

1. Lean Management

Lean is a methodology focused on eliminating waste and improving processes. It originated in manufacturing but has since been applied to virtually every sector. Lean management is based on principles such as:

- **Value stream mapping**: Identifying all the actions (value-creating and non-value-creating) within a process.

- **Eliminating waste**: Waste is anything that doesn't add value to the customer. In Lean, there are seven types of waste: overproduction, waiting, transport, extra processing, inventory, motion, and defects.

- **Continuous improvement (Kaizen)**: Encouraging incremental improvements in processes over time.

What Works:

Lean helps companies streamline their processes and focus on delivering value to customers without unnecessary costs.

Challenges:

Lean requires discipline and a commitment to constant evaluation. In large companies, implementing Lean across different departments can be challenging without a strong cultural buy-in.

2. Six Sigma

Six Sigma is a data-driven methodology aimed at reducing defects and variability in processes. It uses statistical tools to identify root causes of issues and implements solutions to minimize defects and improve quality.

- **DMAIC Framework**: Define, Measure, Analyze, Improve, Control. This process is used for improving existing processes.

- **Data and measurement**: Six Sigma relies heavily on collecting data and using statistical analysis to drive decision-making.

What Works:

Six Sigma is particularly effective in environments where precision and quality control are critical, such as manufacturing, healthcare, and technology.

Challenges:

Six Sigma can sometimes be viewed as too rigid and technical, making it harder to apply in creative or fast-paced environments.

---

3. Total Quality Management (TQM)

Total Quality Management is a holistic approach that involves every employee in the organization. TQM focuses on improving quality at every level of the company, ensuring that everyone is committed to continuous improvement and delivering value to the customer.

- **Customer focus**: Understanding customer needs and aligning processes to meet those needs.

- **Employee involvement**: Engaging everyone in the organization to contribute to quality improvements.

- **Process improvement**: Using data and feedback to constantly evaluate and refine processes.

What Works:

TQM fosters a culture of quality and improvement throughout the organization. It empowers employees at all levels to take ownership of quality.

Challenges:

TQM can be difficult to implement without strong leadership and buy-in from all levels of the organization. The focus on constant improvement can also become overwhelming in organizations that lack the capacity for sustained change.

---

4. Agile Methodology

Agile methodology, initially used in software development, is now being applied in other sectors like marketing, project management, and product development. Agile focuses on flexibility, rapid iteration, and collaboration across cross-functional teams.

- **Iterative work cycles**: Breaking down large projects into smaller, manageable chunks (sprints) with frequent reviews and adjustments.

- **Customer collaboration**: Emphasizing customer feedback and responsiveness over rigid processes.

- **Continuous delivery**: Delivering small, incremental improvements regularly instead of waiting for a final, large product release.

What Works:

Agile is excellent for fast-paced industries where flexibility and customer feedback are crucial for success, like technology and product development.

Challenges:

Implementing Agile outside of software or tech-related fields can be difficult, as it requires a shift in mindset and company structure. Agile can also feel chaotic if not implemented properly.

5. Benchmarking

Benchmarking involves comparing your company's processes and performance metrics to those of industry leaders or competitors. It's a way to identify areas where you can improve and adopt best practices from others.

- **Competitive benchmarking**: Looking at competitors' practices and comparing them to your own to identify gaps in performance.

- **Best practice benchmarking**: Comparing against the highest standards in the industry, even if the comparison is not directly within your sector.

What Works:

Benchmarking provides clear data and insights on where your company stands in comparison to others, allowing you to make informed decisions on how to improve.

Challenges:

While benchmarking can identify gaps, it can sometimes lead to a "me-too" approach without considering your company's unique needs and culture.

The Most Effective Method: A Hybrid Approach

While each of the methods above has its merits, the most effective approach to achieving operational excellence is a **hybrid strategy** that combines elements from multiple methodologies. No single framework can address all aspects of a business, and a tailored approach allows the flexibility to choose the best practices for each department or function within the organization.

The most successful CEOs understand that operational excellence isn't about strictly adhering to one methodology; it's about selecting the right tools for the job and creating a culture of continuous improvement. This involves combining **Lean's waste-reduction focus, Six Sigma's data-driven precision, Agile's**

adaptability, and **TQM's inclusive approach** to ensure that every part of the organization works efficiently and in harmony toward the common goal.

Practical Steps to Develop Operational Excellence

As a CEO, you are the key driver of operational excellence within your organization. Here are some practical steps you can take to develop and implement operational excellence:

1. Assess Your Current Processes

Conduct a thorough assessment of your organization's processes. Identify bottlenecks, inefficiencies, and areas where waste occurs. Engage your team in identifying where improvements can be made.

Practical Tip:

Use value stream mapping to visualize how work flows through your organization. This will help you pinpoint inefficiencies and areas for improvement.

2. Set Clear Objectives for Improvement

Define specific, measurable goals for operational excellence. Whether it's reducing cycle time, improving customer satisfaction, or lowering costs, having clear objectives will guide your improvement efforts.

Practical Tip:

Use the **SMART goals framework** (Specific, Measurable, Achievable, Relevant, Time-bound) to ensure your goals are clearly defined.

3. Foster a Culture of Continuous Improvement

Encourage a mindset of ongoing learning and improvement throughout the company. Provide training on methodologies like Lean or Six Sigma and promote the idea that every employee has a role in improving operations.

Practical Tip:

Establish a **Kaizen** (continuous improvement) culture where small, incremental changes are celebrated. Empower teams to suggest and implement changes.

4. Invest in Technology and Tools

To achieve operational excellence, your company must have the right tools. Invest in technology that streamlines processes, improves data collection, and enables better decision-making.

Practical Tip:

Implement tools like **Enterprise Resource Planning (ERP)** systems, project management software, and data analytics platforms to improve process efficiency.

5. Regularly Review and Adjust

Operational excellence is a journey, not a destination. Regularly review your progress toward your goals, gather feedback, and adjust your strategy as needed.

Practical Tip:

Hold regular performance reviews (e.g., quarterly) where you assess the effectiveness of implemented changes and set new objectives.

Case Study: Jeff Bezos and Amazon's Operational Excellence

One of the best examples of operational excellence in action is **Jeff Bezos and Amazon**. Bezos has always been laser-focused on streamlining Amazon's operations to deliver the best possible experience for customers. From the company's early days, he understood the importance of efficient supply chains, fast delivery, and scalable systems. His obsession with operational excellence has been a key factor in Amazon's success.

Implementing Lean and Data-Driven Decision Making

Bezos instilled a culture of operational excellence by using **Lean principles** to reduce waste and streamline processes. Amazon invested heavily in data and technology to automate and optimize the supply chain. The company's **Fulfilment Centers** are prime examples of operational excellence, leveraging algorithms, robotics, and data analytics to ensure inventory is efficiently managed, and orders are shipped quickly.

Results and Scaling

By focusing on operational excellence, Amazon has been able to scale at an unprecedented rate while maintaining low costs and high customer satisfaction. Its efficiency in inventory management and delivery has allowed Amazon to grow into one of the world's largest companies, disrupting entire industries along the way.

Conclusion: The CEO's Role in Operational Excellence

As a CEO, your role in developing operational excellence cannot be overstated. It requires a strategic approach, a commitment to continuous improvement, and the right leadership to guide your team through the process. By leveraging methodologies like Lean, Six Sigma, Agile, and TQM, and by fostering a culture of accountability, trust, and efficiency, you can position your company to achieve long-term success and operational excellence.

Remember, operational excellence is not a one-time project but an ongoing journey of improvement and adaptation. With the right mindset and tools, you can build a company that not only survives in a competitive marketplace but thrives.

11

Creating Mentorship Programs

In the journey of a successful CEO, one of the most powerful tools for both personal and organizational growth is mentorship. Great leaders understand that their success is not just about their individual knowledge and skills but about how they empower others to reach their full potential. As a CEO, you have the unique opportunity—and responsibility—to build a culture of mentorship within your organization, both for your own development and for the development of your teams.

Mentorship is a process that involves guidance, advice, and support. It's a two-way relationship where knowledge, experience, and wisdom are exchanged, fostering growth for both the mentor and the mentee. In this chapter, we'll explore how mentorship can propel both you and your teams toward success, the various methods executives use to implement mentorship, and practical steps you can take to develop your mentorship skills. Additionally, we'll look at a real-life case study of a CEO who embraced mentorship to build a thriving company.

The Power of Mentorship for CEOs

For many CEOs, mentorship is not just a "nice-to-have" but a strategic tool for personal development and organizational success. As the leader of your company, developing mentorship relationships can:

- **Enhance Your Leadership Skills**: Mentorship provides an opportunity for feedback and reflection, allowing you to improve your decision-making, emotional intelligence, and strategic thinking.

- **Foster Personal Growth**: A mentor can offer a fresh perspective and help you navigate challenges, whether it's scaling your company, managing a crisis, or refining your vision.

- **Develop a Learning Organization**: By creating a mentorship culture, you encourage continuous learning across your organization, helping your teams grow, innovate, and adapt in an ever-changing business environment.

Mentorship, when done well, accelerates both individual and company growth. It allows leaders to move beyond the challenges they face, unlock untapped potential, and build the next generation of leaders within their organization.

Methods Executives Use to Develop Mentorship

There are several approaches CEOs and executives use to develop and implement mentorship, both for themselves and for their teams. Here are a few key methods:

1. One-on-One Mentorship

In this traditional approach, a mentor provides personalized advice, guidance, and support to a mentee. The relationship is often long-term and focused on professional and personal development. The mentor shares their experiences, provides valuable insights, and challenges the mentee to grow.

- **What Works**: One-on-one mentorship provides deep, tailored advice, allowing mentees to receive guidance specific to their needs.

- **Challenges**: This method can be time-consuming for both parties and may not be scalable for larger teams.

Tip:

For busy CEOs, schedule regular, focused meetings with a few select mentees, allowing for deep, meaningful exchanges.

2. Group Mentorship

In group mentorship, a mentor works with a group of individuals, often in a structured setting, to guide them toward their goals. This can be effective for addressing common challenges faced by team members or for fostering a learning environment within a company.

- **What Works**: Group mentorship allows mentees to learn from one another and develop camaraderie, while the mentor can provide insights to the entire group at once.

- **Challenges**: The mentoring may be less personalized, as it is challenging to meet the unique needs of each individual in a larger group.

Tip:

Consider organizing **quarterly group mentorship sessions** where you address key business challenges that are relevant to multiple people or teams.

3. Reverse Mentorship

Reverse mentorship flips the traditional model on its head. In reverse mentorship, younger or less-experienced employees mentor senior executives. This method is especially valuable for CEOs looking to understand new technologies, trends, and the perspectives of younger generations in the workplace.

- **What Works**: Reverse mentorship allows senior leaders to stay in touch with emerging trends and technologies and helps them understand the needs and viewpoints of younger generations.

- **Challenges**: It can be challenging for senior leaders to embrace the idea of being mentored by younger employees, and it requires a high level of openness and humility.

4. Peer Mentorship

Peer mentorship involves executives mentoring one another. CEOs often benefit from having a peer mentor or group of peers with whom they can discuss strategies, challenges, and opportunities. Peer mentorship fosters collaboration and can be extremely effective for mutual growth.

- **What Works**: Peer mentorship provides a level of equality and trust, where both parties can share challenges and brainstorm solutions together.

- **Challenges**: Without clear boundaries, peer mentorship can sometimes devolve into casual discussions rather than focused, purposeful mentorship.

5. Mentorship Programs within the Organization

A formalized mentorship program within your company can help create a culture of development. These programs match junior employees with more experienced leaders in the company. When implemented well, they can accelerate employee growth and align the development of your team with the company's goals.

- **What Works**: Structured mentorship programs allow companies to develop a leadership pipeline, ensuring that knowledge and skills are passed down to future leaders.

- **Challenges**: If not properly managed, these programs can become too rigid or fail to match mentors and mentees with complementary goals or personalities.

Tip:

Implement a **formal mentorship program** within your company, but ensure it has flexibility to evolve based on individual needs and business changes.

The Most Effective Method: A Combination of Approaches

While each method has its strengths, the most effective way to develop mentorship in your organization is through a **hybrid approach** that combines one-on-one mentorship, group mentorship, and peer mentorship. By blending different methods, you can ensure that mentorship is scalable, inclusive, and impactful across your entire company.

A hybrid approach works best because it allows for flexibility and personalization while fostering a collaborative learning culture. You can pair experienced executives with junior leaders, encourage reverse mentorship to stay connected to younger generations, and foster peer-to-peer relationships among your leadership team.

Practical Steps to Develop Your Mentorship Skills

As a CEO, developing mentorship skills is essential for both your personal growth and the success of your team. Here are some practical steps to help you develop and refine your mentorship abilities:

1. Identify Areas for Personal Growth

To be an effective mentor, it's important to understand your own strengths and areas for growth. Seek mentorship yourself from trusted advisors or peers to continually improve your leadership skills.

Tip:

Regularly ask for feedback from your team and mentor network to identify areas where you can grow as a mentor.

2. Set Clear Expectations

Whether you're mentoring one person or a group, set clear expectations from the start. Define what success looks like for both you and your mentee(s), and establish how often you will meet, the topics you will cover, and how progress will be measured.

Tip:

Create a **mentorship contract** with clear goals and outcomes for the relationship to help both you and your mentee stay focused.

3. Listen More Than You Speak

One of the most powerful skills a mentor can have is listening. Give your mentees the space to share their challenges, ideas, and concerns. Your role is to guide, not to give all the answers. Ask thoughtful questions to help them arrive at their own solutions.

Tip:

Practice active listening—don't interrupt and avoid jumping in with solutions too quickly. Instead, ask open-ended questions to encourage reflection.

4. Foster a Growth Mindset

Encourage a growth mindset within yourself and your mentees. Remind them that challenges are opportunities for growth, and failures are stepping stones to success. Show vulnerability by sharing your own learning experiences, including both successes and failures.

Tip:

Celebrate progress over perfection. Acknowledge small wins, and make sure your mentees know it's okay to make mistakes as long as they learn from them.

5. Create a Learning Culture in Your Organization

Develop a culture where mentorship is valued at all levels. Encourage employees to seek out mentors, provide resources for leadership development, and ensure that mentorship is a priority.

Tip:

Regularly highlight successful mentorship stories in company meetings or internal communications to inspire others.

Case Study: Howard Schultz and Starbucks' Mentorship Culture

A great example of a CEO who embraced mentorship to drive corporate growth is **Howard Schultz**, the former CEO of Starbucks. Schultz recognized the importance of mentorship early on in his tenure and made it a cornerstone of Starbucks' success.

Mentorship as a Leadership Development Tool

Schultz implemented a mentorship culture within Starbucks, where senior leaders mentored employees at all levels. He personally mentored many key executives, including former COO Troy Alstead, who later helped guide Starbucks through major expansions and innovations.

Empowering Others Through Mentorship

Schultz also emphasized reverse mentorship. As Starbucks expanded globally, younger employees helped Schultz and his leadership team understand the needs and preferences of a new generation of customers, especially in markets like China and Asia.

The Results

Starbucks' commitment to mentorship helped build a leadership pipeline that allowed the company to scale successfully. The company's culture of mentorship fostered employee loyalty, innovation, and personal development, all of which contributed to its continued growth and global success.

Conclusion: Mentorship is a Critical Leadership Skill for CEOs

As a CEO, developing mentorship for yourself and your teams is a powerful way to drive both personal and organizational growth. By creating a mentorship culture, you not only help individuals reach their full potential but also lay the foundation for a resilient and innovative company. Mentorship is an ongoing process—one that requires commitment, empathy, and a dedication to continuous learning.

By embracing mentorship and cultivating these relationships, you'll not only improve your own leadership but also build a strong, empowered workforce capable of taking your company to new heights.

12

Personal Branding

In today's business world, being a CEO is about more than just leading a company; it's about cultivating an identity that resonates both inside and outside your organization. This is where **personal branding** comes into play. As a CEO, your personal brand shapes how you are perceived, influences your relationships, and plays a significant role in the success of your company.

Your personal brand is how you present yourself—your values, leadership style, expertise, and personality—both in public and within your organization. It's how people perceive you as a leader, and it directly impacts your credibility, trustworthiness, and influence.

In this chapter, we will explore what personal branding is, why it's critical for modern CEOs, and how you can develop and refine your personal brand. We'll also take a look at a real-life case study to demonstrate how a CEO's personal brand can have a profound impact on their career and company.

What is Personal Branding?

Personal branding is the process of establishing and managing your own identity in the marketplace. It's about shaping how others see you, highlighting your strengths, values, and unique qualities that set you apart from others in your field.

For a CEO, your personal brand goes beyond just professional skills; it encompasses your **leadership style**, **communication skills**, **vision**, and even your **values** and **beliefs**. A well-defined personal brand helps you build a following, attract top talent, connect with investors, and even influence the public's perception of your company.

In the past, CEOs were often seen as faceless corporate leaders, but today's most successful executives understand the power of building a personal brand that aligns with their business objectives and their personal values. Your brand shapes how your employees feel about working for you, how customers feel about buying from your company, and how investors feel about trusting you with their capital.

Why Personal Branding Matters for a CEO

1. Attracting Talent and Building Trust

A strong personal brand helps you attract and retain the best talent. Today's workforce, especially millennials and Gen Z, is drawn to leaders who have a clear sense of purpose, authenticity, and vision. Employees are more likely to stay with a company if they respect and admire the CEO and believe in the mission.

Example: Employees at companies with a strong CEO personal brand tend to feel more engaged and aligned with the company's vision and values. A CEO's brand can become a cornerstone of your company's employee value proposition (EVP).

2. Building Credibility with Customers

In the digital age, consumers want to feel connected to the companies they do business with. A CEO with a well-established personal brand can humanize the company, create emotional connections with customers, and build trust. When customers feel they know you, they are more likely to become loyal advocates for your brand.

3. Attracting Investors and Partners

Investors are not just investing in a business—they're investing in a leader. Your personal brand impacts how potential investors view your ability to lead and scale the company. A CEO with a strong personal brand has the power to influence potential investors, partners, and stakeholders.

4. Crisis Management

In moments of crisis, a CEO's personal brand can be a powerful tool for managing the narrative. A respected CEO can help guide a company through difficult times, reassure stakeholders, and retain employee morale. Conversely, a weak or negative personal brand can exacerbate a crisis.

5. Thought Leadership and Industry Influence

Personal branding gives you the platform to become a thought leader in your industry. Whether through public speaking, writing articles, or engaging on social media, your personal brand can help you shape public discourse, influence policy, and drive industry trends.

Practical Steps to Develop Your Personal Brand

Developing a strong personal brand as a CEO is not a one-time effort. It's a continuous process of self-reflection, consistency, and communication. Here are practical steps to help you craft and refine your personal brand:

1. Define Your Core Values and Leadership Philosophy

Your personal brand begins with self-awareness. What do you stand for? What are your core beliefs? Your personal values shape how you lead and interact with others. Take time to reflect on your leadership philosophy and what makes you unique.

Action Step:

Write down your **top five core values**. These should align with both your personal principles and the values you want to promote within your company. Your brand should always reflect these values in every public interaction.

2. Be Authentic

Authenticity is key to a successful personal brand. People are drawn to leaders who are genuine and transparent. Avoid trying to be someone you're not. Be consistent in your message, stay true to your beliefs, and never compromise on your values. Your authenticity will earn the respect and trust of both your team and the public.

Action Step:

Engage in open, honest conversations. Share personal stories and experiences that reflect your values and leadership style, both in private meetings and public speaking opportunities.

3. Communicate Consistently

Your personal brand won't develop on its own. You need to consistently communicate it—whether it's through social media, speaking engagements, interviews, or your company's public-facing communications. Share your thoughts on leadership, innovation, and the future of your industry.

Action Step:

Develop a content strategy for sharing your personal brand across platforms. Use LinkedIn, Twitter, or industry blogs to regularly post content that reflects your expertise, values, and vision.

4. Invest in Thought Leadership

Becoming a recognized thought leader is one of the most powerful ways to build your personal brand. Share your knowledge, speak at industry events, write articles, or participate in podcasts. As you establish yourself as a thought leader, your personal brand will gain visibility and authority.

Action Step:

Commit to contributing to at least one or two thought-leadership initiatives each month, whether it's writing an article, speaking at a conference, or appearing on a podcast.

5. Be Visible in the Right Spaces

In addition to creating content, position yourself in front of key audiences. Engage with industry influencers, build relationships with media outlets, and become involved in causes that align with your personal and professional values. Visibility is key to expanding your influence.

Action Step:

Seek out speaking opportunities at major conferences, join relevant professional organizations, and participate in charitable activities that resonate with your values.

6. Be Transparent During Challenges

Crisis situations present the perfect opportunity to strengthen your personal brand. How you handle challenges, communicate with employees, and interact with the public will define your personal brand. Be open and transparent about issues, and take accountability for both successes and failures.

Action Step:

In times of crisis or difficulty, make sure your message is clear, empathetic, and aligned with your values. Show leadership by making tough decisions with integrity and openness.

Case Study: Richard Branson and the Virgin Brand

One of the most successful examples of a CEO leveraging personal branding is **Richard Branson**, the founder of the Virgin Group. Branson has built a personal brand that is synonymous with adventure, innovation, and boldness. His persona as an unconventional, daring entrepreneur has become integral to Virgin's identity.

Building the Brand

Branson's personal brand has been incredibly effective in aligning with the Virgin Group's business goals. His public persona as a risk-taker and visionary is reflected in Virgin's branding, making the company stand out as a challenger in the industries it serves. Branson's charisma, sense of humor, and willingness to take on daring challenges (such as attempting to fly around the world in a hot air balloon) have made him a global celebrity and a symbol of the Virgin brand.

Leveraging Social Media and Public Appearances

Branson has used social media, books, and public speaking engagements to strengthen his personal brand. His presence on platforms like Twitter, where he engages with fans and shares his experiences, has humanized him and made him relatable to a global audience.

Impact on Virgin Group

Branson's personal brand has had a direct impact on Virgin's success. His ability to attract attention and create buzz has helped Virgin expand into new markets, launch innovative products, and recruit top talent. His personal brand is integral to Virgin's marketing strategy, and it continues to draw customers and investors who are attracted to Branson's values and leadership style.

Conclusion: Building Your Personal Brand as a CEO

As a CEO, your personal brand is one of the most powerful assets you have. It shapes how your employees view you, how customers perceive your company, and how investors and partners engage with your business. By defining your core values, being authentic, and consistently communicating your message, you can build a personal brand that supports both your leadership goals and your company's success.

Remember, personal branding is not a one-time effort; it's an ongoing process that requires dedication, consistency, and authenticity. By investing in your personal brand, you're not only building your career—you're also setting your company up for long-term success.

13

Growing Network Relationships

A s a CEO, one of your most powerful tools for achieving success is networking. While many people view networking as a superficial exchange of business cards, for a CEO, it's much more than that. Networking is about building meaningful relationships that open doors to new opportunities, create alliances, and offer support when challenges arise. It's about surrounding yourself with people who can provide insights, advice, and potential collaborations that help your business grow and thrive.

In this chapter, we will explore the importance of networking, how to network effectively for career success, and the tools and strategies that can help you build a robust network. We'll also dive into a real-life case study of a CEO who leveraged networking to accelerate both their career and the growth of their company.

Why Networking Matters for a CEO

In today's interconnected world, no leader operates in isolation. Networking plays a pivotal role in a CEO's ability to lead effectively, drive innovation, and secure critical resources for business success. Here are some of the key reasons why networking is essential for a CEO:

1. Access to New Opportunities

Networking opens doors to opportunities that might not be immediately visible through traditional channels. Whether it's finding new customers, business partners, investors, or even future employees, your network can provide a wealth of leads and connections that can propel your company forward.

2. Building Trust and Credibility

A well-established network increases your credibility within your industry and beyond. When people know you, respect you, and trust you, they are more likely to recommend your company, give you advice, or partner with you. Building these connections often starts with one-on-one relationships that grow over time.

3. Knowledge and Insight

Networking is a powerful way to gain new insights and knowledge from other industry leaders and experts. By exchanging ideas with your peers, you can keep your finger on the pulse of trends, best practices, and emerging opportunities. This can be especially valuable when navigating challenges or making strategic decisions.

4. Emotional Support and Mentorship

Being a CEO can be a lonely job. Having a network of trusted advisors, mentors, and peers to lean on provides valuable emotional support and guidance. These relationships can help you gain perspective, provide advice during tough decisions, and offer encouragement when things are difficult.

5. Strategic Partnerships and Collaborations

Through networking, you can form strategic partnerships with other companies or individuals that complement your own business. These collaborations can unlock new revenue streams, expand your market reach, and provide access to new technologies or expertise that can drive your company's success.

How to Network for Career Success

Effective networking is not about collecting as many contacts as possible—it's about cultivating meaningful, long-lasting relationships. Here are strategies to help you network like a successful CEO:

1. Focus on Quality, Not Quantity

It's easy to get caught up in the idea of having a large network. However, what truly matters is the quality of those relationships. A few strong, meaningful connections will be far more beneficial than hundreds of superficial ones. Aim to develop relationships with people who share your values and can offer real value in your personal or professional life.

Action Step:

Identify the key individuals who can support your growth as a CEO—industry leaders, mentors, peers, or potential collaborators. Cultivate deeper relationships with these individuals through regular interaction, shared experiences, and mutual support.

2. Attend Industry Events and Conferences

Industry events are a prime opportunity for CEOs to meet and connect with other business leaders. Whether it's a conference, panel discussion, or networking lunch, these gatherings provide a space for like-minded individuals to exchange ideas, solve problems, and build relationships.

Action Step:

Commit to attending at least one major industry event each quarter. Prioritize events where you can engage with key stakeholders, potential clients, or investors. Be intentional about your time—focus on making meaningful connections rather than collecting a stack of business cards.

3. Leverage Social Media and Online Platforms

Today's digital tools, particularly LinkedIn, Twitter, and other professional networking platforms, offer unparalleled opportunities to network with global peers and industry leaders. By sharing your insights, engaging in discussions, and connecting with others online, you can build your digital presence and grow your network without leaving your office.

Action Step:

Invest time in optimizing your LinkedIn profile. Share valuable content and engage in meaningful discussions within groups relevant to your industry. Reach out to individuals whose work you admire and propose a virtual coffee chat or collaboration.

4. Nurture Existing Relationships

Networking isn't just about meeting new people; it's about maintaining and nurturing the relationships you already have. Regular follow-ups, sending thoughtful messages, and finding ways to support others in your network can strengthen your existing connections and lead to new opportunities.

Action Step:

Schedule monthly or quarterly check-ins with key people in your network. This could be a simple email, a LinkedIn message, or even a coffee meeting. Make it a point to offer value in return, whether it's through advice, a referral, or sharing a useful resource.

5. Be a Connector

Successful CEOs often serve as connectors within their networks, linking people together who can benefit from each other's expertise. By helping others in your network, you not only strengthen your relationships but also position yourself as a valuable resource.

Action Step:

Take note of opportunities to introduce people in your network who could collaborate. Connecting two like-minded individuals not only helps them but also solidifies your role as a central figure in your network.

6. Offer Value First

The best networking relationships are built on a foundation of mutual benefit. When you reach out to someone new or reconnect with someone in your network, always offer something of value—whether it's a helpful article, an insightful conversation, or an introduction to someone they may find useful.

Action Step:

Before you ask for anything, think about how you can help the person you're connecting with. Whether it's offering your expertise or connecting them with someone in your network, always focus on adding value first.

Networking Tools and Resources

To maximize your networking potential, you can leverage several tools that streamline the process of connecting with people and managing relationships. Here are some useful tools to help you build and maintain your network:

- **LinkedIn**: The go-to platform for professional networking. It's ideal for connecting with people in your industry, sharing content, and building your personal brand.

- **CRM Systems**: Tools like **HubSpot** or **Salesforce** can help you manage relationships and track important interactions, ensuring you don't lose touch with key contacts.

- **Networking Apps**: Apps like **Shapr** or **Bumble Bizz** allow you to connect with professionals in your area or industry, similar to dating apps but for business connections.

- **Event Platforms**: Platforms like **Eventbrite** or **Meetup** help you discover industry-specific networking events, conferences, and seminars.

- **Personal Branding Platforms**: Websites like **Medium** or **Substack** allow you to share your thoughts, establish yourself as a thought leader, and attract people to your network.

Case Study: Richard Branson and the Power of Networking

Richard Branson, the founder of Virgin Group, has long been recognized for his remarkable ability to build a network of powerful and influential people. Branson's personal brand and his success in scaling Virgin have been built not just on his business acumen, but also on his talent for building relationships.

Strategic Networking for Growth

From early in his career, Branson understood the importance of networking. He started by surrounding himself with a group of trusted advisors and mentors who helped him navigate the complex business world. In the 1970s, Branson used his network to expand Virgin's brand from a small record store into a global music label.

As Virgin grew, Branson used networking to forge partnerships with influential figures in the entertainment, finance, and media industries. For example, Branson famously networked with **Sir Richard Attenborough**, a prominent British film director, to secure an initial investment for Virgin Records. This partnership proved crucial in Virgin's early success.

Building Long-Lasting Relationships

Branson's networking didn't stop with business transactions; he built strong personal relationships with key figures in his network, fostering a sense of camaraderie and trust. He invested time and energy in **mentorships** and **collaborations**, and his ability to connect with people from all walks of life has allowed him to tap into a vast array of resources and ideas.

As a result, Branson's reputation as a visionary leader has helped him secure numerous opportunities, partnerships, and collaborations across different industries, from aviation to telecommunications to space exploration.

Impact on Virgin Group's Success

Branson's extensive network not only gave Virgin Group access to investment and partnerships but also allowed him to leverage key advisors and industry connections to expand into new markets. His network provided him with crucial insights into consumer behavior, emerging trends, and market dynamics, which helped Virgin stay ahead of competitors.

Conclusion: Networking Is an Investment in Your Success

As a CEO, your network is one of your most valuable assets. By consistently investing in building relationships, offering value, and staying connected to people who can support your growth, you're creating opportunities that can propel your career and business forward.

Remember, networking is not a one-time event; it's a lifelong endeavor that requires patience, authenticity, and a willingness to give as much as you receive. With the right approach, your network will not only open doors—it will empower you to achieve the next level of success in your leadership journey.

14

Designing a Strategic Vision

As a CEO, one of your most critical responsibilities is to **set the strategic direction** for your company. Your vision is more than just a guiding light; it's the foundation upon which you will build your company's future. A clear, compelling strategic vision not only aligns your team but also drives your company toward sustained success. Without it, even the most talented teams can struggle to maintain focus, innovation, and growth.

In this chapter, we will discuss the importance of strategic visioning, how to develop a strategic vision, and the tools that can help you create a roadmap for long-term success. We will also explore a real-life case study to show how a CEO's strategic vision transformed a business and led it to new heights.

Why Strategic Vision Matters for a CEO

Strategic visioning is the ability to see beyond the day-to-day operations and understand where the business needs to go in the future. A strategic vision is your **company's North Star**, guiding your decisions, inspiring your team, and positioning the business for growth and resilience. Here are some key reasons why strategic visioning is vital:

1. Provides Direction and Clarity

A strong vision gives your company a clear sense of purpose and direction. When everyone in the organization understands the vision, they can align their efforts toward a common goal. This unity boosts morale, enhances collaboration, and creates a sense of shared purpose.

2. Drives Decision-Making

As a CEO, you'll face countless decisions every day. A clear strategic vision serves as a framework for making those decisions. Whether it's choosing between two new business opportunities or deciding on a major organizational change, your vision will help you prioritize and focus on what matters most.

3. Fosters Innovation and Growth

A well-crafted vision helps your company anticipate change, innovate, and stay ahead of the competition. It pushes you and your team to think creatively about how to solve problems and create new products, services, or experiences that will propel the business forward.

4. Attracts Investment and Talent

Investors, partners, and top talent are attracted to businesses that have a compelling, forward-looking vision. A strong strategic vision signals to the market that your company is serious about growth and long-term success, making it easier to secure funding and build valuable relationships.

How to Develop a Strategic Vision

Creating a strategic vision requires deep reflection, forward thinking, and a clear understanding of both your company's current position and its potential future. Here's how to craft a strategic vision that will help you guide your business successfully:

1. Understand Your Company's Core Purpose and Values

Before you can create a vision for the future, you need to define your company's core purpose. What do you stand for? What problem does your business solve, and for whom? Knowing your company's values and mission is the foundation for any strategic vision, as it will guide your decisions and ensure that the vision stays aligned with your company's culture and long-term goals.

Action Step:

Conduct a strategic planning session with your leadership team to revisit your company's mission and values. Clarify your purpose and ensure that everyone is aligned around it. This foundational understanding will be crucial as you shape your vision.

2. Analyze Market Trends and Industry Dynamics

Your strategic vision must account for both current and future market conditions. This requires you to stay informed about trends and changes within your industry, technology advancements, regulatory shifts, and consumer behavior patterns. Having this knowledge enables you to make informed decisions about where your company can grow and innovate.

Action Step:

Spend time analyzing market research, industry reports, and competitor strategies. Identify emerging trends and think about how your company can either leverage these changes or adapt to them.

3. Define Long-Term Goals and Ambitions

A strategic vision isn't just about what your company will look like next year— it's about where you want to be 5, 10, or even 20 years from now. Define the long-term goals that will propel your company to the next level. These should be bold, but achievable, and aligned with your company's values.

Action Step:

Ask yourself: Where do I want my company to be in 5 years? What are the key milestones that need to happen for us to get there? Write these down as long-term goals and ensure they are measurable and realistic.

4. Engage Stakeholders in the Visioning Process

Developing a strategic vision should not be a solitary exercise. Involve key stakeholders—your leadership team, employees, and trusted advisors—in the process. Their input will give you valuable perspectives and help you identify blind spots. Engaging your team early on in the process also increases buy-in and ensures that everyone is invested in the vision.

Action Step:

Host brainstorming sessions with your leadership team and other key stakeholders. Gather feedback and ideas on where the company should be headed and how best to get there.

5. Develop a Clear, Concise Vision Statement

Once you've gathered insights and defined your goals, distill your vision into a **short, clear, and inspiring vision statement**. This should be a succinct description of where you want your company to go and what you hope to achieve. A good vision statement should be memorable and motivating.

Action Step:

Create a vision statement that clearly articulates your company's future. Keep it simple, aspirational, and focused on the most important long-term outcomes.

6. Align Strategy with Vision

A great vision is only as strong as the strategy behind it. Your vision must be actionable, with specific strategic initiatives designed to achieve it. Break down your vision into key focus areas (such as market expansion, product innovation, operational efficiency) and create a roadmap for how to achieve each one.

Action Step:

Break down your vision into specific, actionable strategic goals for the next 3–5 years. Identify the key actions, timelines, and resources needed to achieve these goals.

Tools for Strategy Development

To build and refine your strategic vision, you can leverage several tools that help guide your thinking and decision-making. Here are some of the most effective tools for strategy development:

1. SWOT Analysis

A **SWOT analysis** (Strengths, Weaknesses, Opportunities, Threats) helps you assess your company's current position in the market and identify areas for growth. This is a foundational tool to understand your internal strengths and weaknesses, as well as the external opportunities and challenges.

2. PESTLE Analysis

A **PESTLE analysis** (Political, Economic, Social, Technological, Legal, Environmental) is a useful tool for analyzing macro-environmental factors that could impact your business in the future. This will help you stay ahead of potential risks and capitalize on emerging opportunities.

3. Visioning Workshops

Conducting visioning workshops with your leadership team and stakeholders is an excellent way to brainstorm, align, and refine your strategic vision. These workshops can help you build consensus, clarify goals, and set priorities for the future.

4. OKRs (Objectives and Key Results)

Once you have your strategic vision, you can break it down into **OKRs** (Objectives and Key Results). OKRs are a powerful framework for setting clear, measurable goals and tracking progress toward your strategic objectives. They help ensure alignment between your vision and your company's day-to-day operations.

Case Study: How Satya Nadella's Vision Transformed Microsoft

One of the most striking examples of effective strategic visioning in recent years is **Satya Nadella's leadership at Microsoft**. When Nadella became CEO in 2014, Microsoft was struggling to adapt to the rapidly changing technology landscape. The company had strong products but was losing ground to more agile, cloud-based competitors like Amazon and Google.

The Vision: "Mobile-First, Cloud-First"

Nadella's strategic vision was bold: He focused on transforming Microsoft into a **cloud-first, mobile-first company**. This vision was a departure from the company's traditional software-centric approach, but it was precisely the shift needed to put Microsoft on a path to growth.

Strategic Actions Taken:

- Nadella spearheaded Microsoft's **move to the cloud**, making Azure a core part of the company's future strategy. He moved Microsoft away from relying solely on Windows and Office, to embracing cloud computing, artificial intelligence, and subscription-based services.

- Under his leadership, Microsoft focused on creating **cross-platform solutions**, making its software and services available on multiple platforms (including Android and iOS). This openness signaled to the market that Microsoft was no longer the old "monolithic" tech giant.

- Nadella also fostered a **culture of innovation** within Microsoft, encouraging employees to embrace new ideas and collaborate more effectively.

Results:

- Microsoft's market value skyrocketed, and the company became one of the most valuable firms in the world.

- Azure became one of the leading cloud computing platforms globally.

- Nadella's vision helped Microsoft become more agile and adaptive in a tech ecosystem that is constantly evolving.

Nadella's success is a clear demonstration of the power of strategic visioning. His ability to see where the technology industry was headed—and position Microsoft accordingly—transformed the company from a software giant to a leader in cloud computing and digital transformation.

Conclusion: Strategic Vision Is the Key to Long-Term Success

As a CEO, developing a compelling strategic vision is essential for guiding your company through uncertainty, adapting to change, and achieving sustained success. Your vision will serve as a rallying cry for your team, a roadmap for your strategy, and a tool for inspiring innovation.

By understanding your company's core purpose, analyzing the market, and aligning your team around a common goal, you can craft a vision that drives meaningful change and accelerates growth. Remember, your vision is not a static destination—it's an ongoing process that evolves as your business grows and adapts to new challenges.

When you lead with a clear, compelling vision, you empower your organization to not just meet the future, but to shape it.

15

The Art of Negotiation

Negotiation is a skill that every CEO must master if they want to lead their company to success. Whether you are securing a partnership, closing a major deal, or managing internal conflicts, the ability to negotiate effectively can be the difference between achieving your objectives or falling short. As a CEO, your negotiation skills will shape your company's future—impacting everything from profitability and market position to company culture and employee satisfaction.

In this chapter, we will explore the importance of negotiation for a CEO, how to develop and refine your negotiation skills, and the tools that can help you become a more effective negotiator. We will also share a real-life case study that demonstrates how a CEO used negotiation to drive significant business outcomes.

Why Negotiation Matters for a CEO

Negotiation isn't just about getting the best deal for your company—it's about building relationships, maintaining trust, and finding mutually beneficial solutions. As the CEO, you'll be involved in negotiations at every level of the organization: from high-stakes mergers to everyday discussions with employees and clients. Here are some reasons why negotiation is a core skill for CEOs:

1. Securing Business Deals and Partnerships

CEOs are frequently responsible for negotiating the terms of major partnerships, acquisitions, and investment deals. The outcome of these negotiations can dramatically affect the company's bottom line, market reach, and future growth potential.

2. Managing Internal Relationships

Negotiation is not limited to external stakeholders. Within your company, you will negotiate with leadership teams, employees, and department heads to align priorities, resolve conflicts, and set strategic goals. The way you handle these internal negotiations can shape your company's culture and employee engagement.

3. Influencing Stakeholders and Investors

CEOs must also negotiate with investors, board members, and other key stakeholders. Being able to effectively present your vision and negotiate terms is crucial for securing funding, gaining support for new initiatives, or navigating corporate governance challenges.

4. Navigating Crisis Situations

During times of crisis—whether due to economic downturns, public relations issues, or supply chain disruptions—CEOs must negotiate with a range of internal and external parties. Strong negotiation skills can help resolve issues quickly and create win-win outcomes that preserve relationships.

5. Creating Win-Win Solutions

The most effective CEOs understand that negotiation is about creating value for all parties involved. Approaching negotiations with a collaborative mindset, rather than a win-lose mentality, leads to better long-term outcomes for your company and stakeholders.

How to Develop Effective Negotiation Skills

Mastering the art of negotiation takes practice, patience, and a keen understanding of human behavior. Here's a step-by-step guide to developing your negotiation skills:

1. Understand Your Objectives

Before entering any negotiation, you need to clearly define what you want to achieve. Having a firm grasp on your company's objectives and what you're willing to compromise on is key to setting a strong foundation for the conversation.

Action Step:

Outline your top three goals before each negotiation. Consider both the "must-haves" (non-negotiables) and the "nice-to-haves" (things you're willing to give up). This will help you stay focused and avoid emotional decision-making.

2. Listen Actively

Effective negotiators understand that listening is just as important as speaking. When you actively listen to the other party's needs and concerns, you build trust and gain valuable insights that can help you reach a mutually beneficial agreement.

Action Step:

Practice **active listening** during your next negotiation. Focus on what the other party is saying without interrupting. Paraphrase or summarize their points to show that you understand their perspective.

3. Build Rapport

Building rapport with the other party can create an atmosphere of trust and cooperation. A strong relationship allows for more open dialogue and can lead to better outcomes for both sides.

Action Step:

Begin each negotiation by finding common ground. This could be a shared interest, a mutual connection, or a common goal. Small gestures, like expressing empathy or showing appreciation, can also help build rapport.

4. Stay Calm Under Pressure

Negotiations can become tense, especially when stakes are high. Staying calm and composed allows you to think clearly, manage emotions, and make rational decisions. Reacting emotionally can damage relationships and jeopardize the outcome.

Action Step:

Practice stress-reduction techniques, such as deep breathing or mindfulness, before entering high-stakes negotiations. This will help you stay focused and maintain a level-headed approach.

5. Be Prepared to Walk Away

One of the most powerful negotiation tools you have is the ability to walk away if the deal isn't right. By knowing your walk-away point—whether it's a price, terms, or conditions—you ensure that you don't make concessions that could harm your company.

Action Step:

Determine your "BATNA" (Best Alternative to a Negotiated Agreement) before entering negotiations. If the terms don't align with your needs, be prepared to walk away and explore other opportunities.

6. Find Creative Solutions

Great negotiators don't just settle for compromise—they seek creative solutions that benefit both parties. This often involves thinking outside the box and finding innovative ways to resolve conflicts or meet the needs of all parties involved.

Action Step:

During negotiations, think about potential "win-win" solutions. Consider how you can meet the other party's needs while also advancing your company's objectives. Brainstorm creative alternatives if you hit an impasse.

Tools for Successful Negotiation

Several tools and frameworks can enhance your ability to negotiate successfully. Here are some of the most effective:

1. BATNA (Best Alternative to a Negotiated Agreement)

This is a key negotiation concept that helps you understand your options if a deal falls through. Having a strong BATNA gives you leverage in negotiations and prevents you from settling for unfavorable terms.

2. ZOPA (Zone of Possible Agreement)

ZOPA refers to the range in which both parties can agree. Understanding where your ZOPA overlaps with the other party's allows you to focus on finding a middle ground that benefits both sides.

3. The 7-38-55 Rule

This rule, developed by psychologist Albert Mehrabian, suggests that in face-to-face communication:

- **7%** of communication comes from words.

- **38%** comes from tone of voice.

- **55%** comes from body language. Being aware of non-verbal cues can help you understand what the other party is truly thinking and feeling during the negotiation.

4. Negotiation Leverage

Knowing where you have leverage is key to influencing the outcome. This could be based on your company's financial position, market power, or unique value proposition. Understanding your leverage allows you to negotiate with confidence.

5. Anchoring Technique

This involves starting the negotiation with an initial offer that sets the tone for the discussion. Research shows that the first offer often serves as an anchor point for the negotiation process, influencing the final agreement.

Real-Life Case Study: How Howard Schultz Used Negotiation to Build Starbucks

Howard Schultz, the former CEO of Starbucks, is a prime example of how effective negotiation can drive business growth. Schultz took a small coffee shop and transformed it into a global coffee empire. Central to his success was his ability to negotiate deals with suppliers, real estate owners, and investors that laid the foundation for Starbucks' rapid expansion.

Negotiating with Real Estate Partners

In the early days of Starbucks' expansion, Schultz negotiated leases with landlords to secure prime real estate locations for Starbucks stores. The company's success was heavily dependent on finding the right locations to build brand recognition. Schultz's negotiating ability helped him secure key locations in high-traffic areas, often beating out competitors.

Strategic Approach:

Schultz didn't just focus on the financial terms of the leases—he also negotiated with landlords to create mutually beneficial agreements. For example, he often worked out terms that allowed Starbucks to share in the revenue of mall-based locations, which helped reduce risk for both parties.

Negotiating with Coffee Bean Suppliers

Another critical negotiation was with coffee bean suppliers. As Starbucks grew, it needed a consistent supply of high-quality coffee beans to meet demand. Schultz negotiated long-term contracts with farmers and suppliers to ensure that Starbucks could maintain its product quality at scale.

Strategic Approach:

Schultz built relationships with suppliers, focusing on sustainable sourcing practices. By negotiating with an emphasis on ethical sourcing and long-term partnerships, he ensured that Starbucks not only secured quality coffee beans but also built a reputation as a socially responsible brand.

Negotiating with Investors

When Starbucks went public, Schultz needed to negotiate with investors to secure capital for expansion. He used his compelling vision of Starbucks as a global brand to persuade investors that the company was a worthwhile investment, despite the risks involved.

Strategic Approach:

Schultz communicated a clear vision of Starbucks as more than just a coffee shop—it was a "third place" where people could gather outside of their home and work. This vision resonated with investors and helped Starbucks secure the funding needed to expand globally.

Conclusion: Negotiation Is Key to CEO Success

As a CEO, mastering negotiation is essential for achieving both short-term goals and long-term success. By developing a deep understanding of your objectives, listening actively, building rapport, and using strategic tools, you can become a more effective negotiator. Strong negotiation skills not only help you close deals—they also build trust, create win-win outcomes, and strengthen relationships that drive your company forward.

By following the steps outlined in this chapter and learning from real-life examples like Howard Schultz, you can hone your negotiation abilities and use them to shape the future of your company. Remember, negotiation is not just about getting what you want—it's about creating value and building lasting partnerships that will sustain your success for years to come.

16

Emotional Intelligence

As a CEO, your ability to lead is not just about making tough decisions, driving profitability, or setting strategies. It's about understanding and managing emotions—both your own and those of your team. This skill, often referred to as **Emotional Intelligence (EQ)**, is crucial for building relationships, motivating employees, resolving conflicts, and creating a productive, healthy company culture.

In this chapter, we will explore why emotional intelligence is essential for effective leadership, how to develop your emotional intelligence, and provide practical steps to help you enhance this critical skill. We will also dive into a real-life case study to illustrate how a CEO's emotional intelligence shaped their leadership style and led their company to success.

Why Emotional Intelligence Matters for a CEO

Emotional intelligence is the ability to recognize, understand, and manage your own emotions, as well as the emotions of others. For a CEO, this means being able to navigate complex interpersonal dynamics, make decisions that consider both logic and emotions, and foster an environment where people feel heard, valued, and motivated.

1. Building Strong Relationships

A CEO with high emotional intelligence is better equipped to build and maintain strong relationships with employees, stakeholders, clients, and investors. Understanding and empathizing with others' emotions allows you to connect on a deeper level and resolve conflicts more effectively.

2. Creating a Positive Company Culture

Your emotional intelligence sets the tone for your organization's culture. A CEO who is self-aware and empathetic will create an environment where open communication, trust, and collaboration flourish. This, in turn, leads to higher employee satisfaction, retention, and productivity.

3. Enhancing Decision-Making

Leaders with strong emotional intelligence are able to make decisions that balance both logic and emotion. They are not swayed by fleeting feelings or external pressures, but instead are able to stay grounded and make choices that align with the company's values and long-term vision.

4. Managing Stress and Crisis Situations

In times of stress or crisis, emotional intelligence allows CEOs to remain calm and composed. This ability to manage their own emotions while understanding the emotional state of their team enables them to guide the company through challenges without losing focus or perspective.

5. Motivating and Inspiring Teams

High EQ leaders are able to inspire and motivate their teams through empathy, active listening, and by providing emotional support. They know how to celebrate wins, provide constructive feedback, and lift people up when they face setbacks. This motivates employees to perform at their best and align their personal goals with the company's mission.

The Five Components of Emotional Intelligence

Emotional intelligence is not a single trait but a set of skills that can be developed over time. According to psychologist Daniel Goleman, who popularized the concept of EQ, there are five key components:

1. Self-Awareness

Self-awareness is the ability to recognize and understand your own emotions, strengths, weaknesses, values, and how they affect others. When you are self-aware, you are more in control of your reactions and can make better decisions.

2. Self-Regulation

Self-regulation refers to your ability to control your emotions and behaviors, especially in stressful situations. It involves staying calm and composed, avoiding impulsive reactions, and managing negative emotions like frustration or anger.

3. Motivation

Highly emotionally intelligent leaders are self-motivated and passionate about their work. They maintain a positive attitude even in the face of setbacks and have a strong drive to achieve goals. They also inspire the same motivation in their teams.

4. Empathy

Empathy is the ability to recognize, understand, and share the feelings of others. For a CEO, empathy is crucial for building trust and fostering a collaborative environment. Empathetic leaders are better at conflict resolution, communication, and understanding their team's needs.

5. Social Skills

Social skills involve the ability to build and manage relationships. This includes communication, conflict management, teamwork, and leadership. Leaders with strong social skills are effective communicators, able to influence others positively and resolve conflicts in a constructive way.

How to Develop Emotional Intelligence

Emotional intelligence is not an innate trait—it's a skill that can be developed with intention and practice. Here's how you can cultivate each component of emotional intelligence:

1. Develop Self-Awareness

- **Regular Reflection**: Take time to reflect on your emotions, thoughts, and behaviors. Journaling or mindfulness practices can help you gain insights into how you react in different situations and how these reactions impact your leadership.

- **Seek Feedback**: Ask colleagues, mentors, or team members for honest feedback on how you come across in different situations. This will help you become more aware of how your emotions affect others.

- **Mindfulness Practices**: Meditation, breathing exercises, and other mindfulness techniques can help you become more aware of your emotional state and learn how to manage it more effectively.

Action Step:

Spend 10 minutes at the end of each day reflecting on your emotional responses. Did you react impulsively to any situation? Could you have responded differently? This will help you develop greater self-awareness.

2. Improve Self-Regulation

- **Pause Before Reacting**: When you feel a strong emotion building up—whether it's anger, frustration, or anxiety—pause and take a deep breath. This will give you time to think before responding.

- **Practice Stress Management**: Engage in activities like exercise, yoga, or journaling that help you manage stress. The more you practice self-regulation, the easier it will become to handle tough situations calmly.

- **Reframe Negative Thoughts**: Challenge negative thoughts and replace them with positive or neutral alternatives. This will help you stay in control of your emotions and not let negativity dictate your behavior.

Action Step:

The next time you feel stressed or frustrated, take a few moments to breathe deeply and ask yourself, "What's the best way to respond to this?" Practicing this pause will help you stay in control.

3. Cultivate Motivation

- **Set Meaningful Goals**: Make sure your personal and professional goals align with your values. When you're motivated by something that resonates with you deeply, you'll be more driven to achieve it.

- **Maintain a Positive Outlook**: Train yourself to focus on the positives, even in difficult situations. When challenges arise, remind yourself of your company's long-term mission and the impact you're trying to make.

- **Celebrate Wins**: Recognize and celebrate milestones—both big and small. This positive reinforcement will help maintain your motivation and inspire your team to stay focused on their goals.

Action Step:

At the start of each week, write down your top three goals for the week. Make sure they are tied to something meaningful. Celebrate progress toward those goals at the end of the week.

4. Practice Empathy

- **Listen Actively**: When interacting with your team, practice active listening. Give them your full attention, acknowledge their feelings, and avoid interrupting.

- **Understand Different Perspectives**: Take time to understand the motivations, feelings, and challenges of others. Walk in their shoes to gain a deeper understanding of their needs and concerns.

- **Show Compassion**: Empathy is not just about understanding others—it's also about responding with kindness and support. Offer help when people are struggling and celebrate their achievements.

Action Step:

The next time you speak with a colleague or team member, focus entirely on what they are saying without distractions. Reflect on their emotions and respond thoughtfully.

5. Develop Social Skills

- **Improve Communication**: Effective communication is at the heart of strong social skills. Practice clear, concise communication, and make sure to actively listen to others.

- **Conflict Resolution**: Learn how to address conflicts constructively. Instead of avoiding tough conversations, approach them with empathy, patience, and a focus on finding solutions.

- **Foster Team Collaboration**: Create an environment where team members feel comfortable working together and sharing ideas. Use your social skills to build strong, effective teams.

Action Step:

Practice your communication skills by regularly checking in with your team. Ask for feedback on your leadership style and listen to suggestions for improvement.

Real-Life Case Study: How Satya Nadella Used Emotional Intelligence to Transform Microsoft

When Satya Nadella took over as CEO of **Microsoft** in 2014, the company was in need of transformation. While Microsoft had strong products, it lacked the agile, innovative mindset needed to thrive in the evolving tech industry. Nadella's leadership style—rooted in emotional intelligence—played a key role in turning Microsoft around.

Empathy and Cultural Transformation

Nadella focused on fostering a culture of **empathy** and collaboration. He recognized that Microsoft's previous "know-it-all" culture needed to shift to a "learn-it-all" mindset, where employees felt supported and encouraged to grow.

By showing empathy toward his employees and leading with humility, Nadella gained their trust and helped shift the company's focus to collaboration and innovation. He worked closely with employees to understand their concerns and create an environment that supported growth and learning.

Self-Regulation and Calm Leadership

During challenging times, such as when Microsoft was facing strong competition from rivals like Amazon and Google, Nadella demonstrated **self-regulation**. He remained calm and focused, never letting external pressures derail the company's long-term vision. His ability to manage stress and stay composed inspired confidence in his leadership.

Inspiring Motivation

Nadella's emotional intelligence also helped him inspire **motivation** within the company. He motivated employees not just through financial incentives, but by making them feel like part of something larger. He often spoke about the company's mission to "empower every person and organization on the planet to achieve more," which resonated deeply with Microsoft employees and helped them align their work with a greater purpose.

Through his leadership, Nadella successfully transformed Microsoft from a technology giant focused on legacy products to a cloud and AI leader with a renewed sense of purpose and innovation.

Conclusion: Emotional Intelligence is the Cornerstone of Effective Leadership

For a CEO, emotional intelligence is not just a "nice-to-have" trait—it is essential for leading with impact and creating lasting business success. By developing self-awareness, self-regulation, empathy, motivation, and strong social skills, you can become a more effective leader, create stronger relationships, and navigate challenges with ease.

Just as Satya Nadella used his emotional intelligence to lead Microsoft through a period of transformation, you too can leverage EQ to create a thriving, high-performing organization. Remember, emotional intelligence is a lifelong skill that can be cultivated over time, and its impact on your leadership and your company's success cannot be overstated.

17

Public Speaking Confidence

As a CEO, one of the most powerful tools in your leadership arsenal is your ability to communicate effectively. Public speaking isn't just about delivering presentations or speeches; it's about inspiring confidence, sharing your vision, and rallying your team and stakeholders around your mission. Whether you're addressing employees, investors, clients, or the media, the way you speak can profoundly impact your leadership and the future of your company.

In this chapter, we'll explore the importance of public speaking in leadership, how to develop public speaking skills, tools to help you practice, and steps you can take to become a more effective speaker. We'll also examine a real-life case study to demonstrate how a CEO used public speaking to impact critical corporate decisions and drive business success.

Why Public Speaking is Crucial for a Successful CEO

Public speaking is not just a skill—it's an essential leadership tool that can influence everything from employee engagement to market perception. Here are some reasons why public speaking is so important for a CEO:

1. Inspiring and Motivating Teams

As a CEO, one of your key responsibilities is to inspire and motivate your team. Public speaking gives you a platform to communicate the company's vision, share progress toward goals, and celebrate achievements. Your words can fuel your team's passion and commitment to the company's success.

2. Building Credibility and Trust

CEOs who speak confidently and authentically establish trust with their employees, clients, and investors. Effective public speaking helps you build your personal brand and demonstrate authority. When you speak clearly and with conviction, people are more likely to believe in your leadership.

3. Shaping Corporate Culture

Through public speaking, you have the power to shape your company's culture. By addressing company values, setting expectations, and creating a shared sense of purpose, you influence the behavior and mindset of your organization. A strong public message can reinforce the culture you want to create.

4. Navigating Crisis Situations

Whether you're facing a financial downturn, a product failure, or a PR crisis, your ability to speak confidently and transparently in public is crucial. The way you communicate during a crisis can help stabilize your team, calm stakeholders, and maintain trust with customers. Clear and empathetic messaging can turn a challenge into an opportunity for growth.

5. Engaging Stakeholders and Investors

Investors and stakeholders want to hear directly from the CEO. Your ability to articulate your company's strategy, financial health, and growth potential in a public setting helps build investor confidence and attracts funding. Public speaking helps you communicate complex ideas in a way that resonates with your audience, whether they are financial experts or everyday customers.

How to Develop Public Speaking Skills

Public speaking is not an innate talent; it's a skill that can be developed with practice, feedback, and intention. Here's how you can hone your public speaking skills to become a more effective communicator:

1. Master the Fundamentals of Public Speaking

Before you even think about stepping on stage, it's important to understand the basic principles of public speaking:

- **Clarity**: Speak clearly and at an appropriate pace. Avoid using jargon or overly complex language.

- **Body Language**: Use purposeful gestures, maintain eye contact, and stand with confidence. Your body language should reinforce your message, not distract from it.

- **Engagement**: Keep your audience engaged by varying your tone, pacing, and delivery style. Don't just read from a script—connect with your audience.

2. Develop a Strong Message

Every speech or presentation should be built around a clear, concise message. The goal is to leave your audience with one central idea or takeaway. Whether you're giving a keynote, a quarterly report, or a crisis address, ensure your message is well-organized and impactful.

- **Structure Your Message**: A typical public speech follows the classic structure:

    o **Introduction**: Hook your audience with an engaging start.

    o **Body**: Present the core ideas with clear examples.

    o **Conclusion**: End with a strong call to action or a summary.

3. Rehearse and Practice

Like any skill, public speaking requires regular practice. The more you practice, the more comfortable you'll become speaking in front of groups.

- **Record Yourself**: Record your speeches or presentations and review them critically. Pay attention to areas where you can improve, such as pacing, tone, and body language.

- **Rehearse in Front of Others**: Practice in front of a colleague, friend, or mentor who can provide constructive feedback.

4. Use Visual Aids and Tools

In many business settings, visual aids (like slides or charts) can help clarify complex ideas and reinforce your message. However, be mindful not to over-rely on them. The key is to use them as a supplement to your speech, not as a crutch.

- **PowerPoint/Keynote**: Use visual aids to outline key points or share important data.

- **Teleprompters**: If you're delivering a scripted speech, a teleprompter can help you stay on track without losing eye contact with your audience.

5. Overcome Public Speaking Anxiety

Almost everyone experiences some level of anxiety before speaking in public. To manage this, practice relaxation techniques such as deep breathing, visualization, or mindfulness. Focus on the message rather than the audience's judgment.

Toastmasters: A Valuable Resource for Aspiring Speakers

One of the most effective ways to develop public speaking skills is to participate in a group like **Toastmasters International**, a global organization that helps individuals improve their communication and leadership skills.

Toastmasters provides a supportive environment where you can:

- **Practice Regularly**: Deliver speeches in a low-pressure setting, receive feedback, and gradually improve.

- **Receive Constructive Feedback**: Toastmasters members offer specific feedback that helps you identify your strengths and areas for improvement.

- **Build Confidence**: The more you speak, the more comfortable you'll become with public speaking.

Toastmasters is an excellent resource for CEOs who want to improve their public speaking skills in a structured, supportive environment.

Practical Steps to Improve Your Public Speaking

Here are practical steps you can take to develop your public speaking skills:

1. **Start Small**: Begin by speaking in front of small groups. This could be a team meeting or a lunch with colleagues. Gradually increase the size of your audience as you build confidence.

2. **Know Your Audience**: Tailor your message to your audience's interests, knowledge level, and needs. Whether speaking to investors, employees, or clients, your message should resonate with them on a personal level.

3. **Prepare Thoroughly**: Don't just show up and wing it. Write your speech or presentation in advance, and rehearse it multiple times. The more prepared you are, the more confident you'll feel.

4. **Seek Feedback**: After delivering a speech, ask for feedback from colleagues, mentors, or team members. Constructive criticism is crucial for growth, so use it to refine your delivery.

5. **Join a Speaking Group**: As mentioned earlier, joining a group like Toastmasters can provide ongoing practice and support as you develop your speaking skills.

6. **Take a Public Speaking Course**: Consider taking a course on public speaking to deepen your skills. Many organizations offer workshops or

online programs that provide in-depth training on presentation techniques, voice modulation, and body language.

Real-Life Case Study: Howard Schultz and the Role of Public Speaking in Starbucks' Growth

Howard Schultz, the former CEO of **Starbucks**, is a prime example of how public speaking can be used effectively to drive corporate growth and impact. Schultz, known for his charismatic and authentic speaking style, used public speaking to rally employees, share the company's vision, and navigate challenges.

Inspiring Employees with a Vision

Schultz understood that Starbucks was not just a coffee company; it was a place where people could come together, experience community, and have meaningful interactions. He often used public speaking to share this vision with employees, helping them connect to the company's core values. His ability to inspire and motivate through public speaking played a key role in building employee loyalty and engagement.

Facing Crisis with Confidence

During the 2008 financial crisis, Starbucks faced significant challenges, including declining sales and rising costs. Schultz used public speaking to address employees directly, communicate the company's strategy for recovery, and instill confidence. He didn't shy away from discussing the tough issues but spoke with transparency and conviction. His ability to connect emotionally with his employees helped the company stay focused and united during difficult times.

External Stakeholder Engagement

Schultz also used public speaking to engage external stakeholders. When Starbucks was seeking to expand globally, Schultz delivered speeches that communicated the company's long-term strategy, the importance of ethical sourcing, and its commitment to social responsibility. These speeches helped build trust with investors, customers, and the broader community, supporting Starbucks' growth into one of the most recognized global brands.

Conclusion: Mastering Public Speaking for Leadership Success

Public speaking is an indispensable skill for any CEO who wants to lead with influence, motivate their team, and drive their company to success. By mastering public speaking, you can communicate your vision, address challenges head-on, and build credibility with your stakeholders. With practice, feedback, and the right tools—like Toastmasters—you can refine your public speaking skills and use them to create lasting impact.

Remember, as a CEO, your words matter. When you speak with confidence, clarity, and empathy, you not only shape your company's future but also inspire those around you to join you on that journey.

18

Leadership Ethics

In today's business landscape, success is no longer just about profit margins, market share, or innovation. More than ever, it's about **ethics**—how a CEO leads, how decisions are made, and how the company engages with its employees, customers, and communities. A leader's ethical principles shape corporate culture, influence brand reputation, and create lasting value. Ethical leadership is foundational to sustainable success, and a CEO's actions set the tone for the entire organization.

In this chapter, we will explore the importance of leadership ethics, how to develop ethical leadership skills, and the role of diversity, equity, and inclusion (DEI) and environmental, social, and governance (ESG) in fostering an ethical business environment. We will also provide practical steps to help you develop and implement ethical leadership principles, along with a real-life case study of a CEO who used ethical leadership to drive corporate growth.

Why Leadership Ethics Matter

1. Building Trust and Credibility

Ethics in leadership is directly tied to trust—trust from employees, customers, investors, and other stakeholders. When a CEO leads with integrity, transparency, and accountability, they create a culture of trust that permeates throughout the organization. Trust is the bedrock upon which all other relationships are built, and it is essential for long-term business success.

2. Long-Term Sustainability

Ethical leadership is not about short-term gains. It's about making decisions that sustain the organization's reputation, growth, and impact over the long run.

Ethical decisions may not always yield immediate profits, but they build a solid foundation that ensures the company's resilience in the face of challenges, crises, and market fluctuations.

3. Employee Engagement and Retention

Employees want to work for organizations they can be proud of. Ethical leadership inspires loyalty, boosts morale, and increases employee engagement. When employees believe in the ethical principles of their CEO and feel that their work aligns with a higher purpose, they are more likely to stay with the company and contribute to its success.

4. Customer Loyalty and Brand Reputation

In an age where information is readily available, customers are more discerning than ever about the brands they choose to support. Companies that lead with strong ethical values—such as fairness, honesty, and responsibility—attract customers who share those values. Ethical leadership enhances a company's brand reputation, fosters customer loyalty, and differentiates the brand in competitive markets.

5. Attracting Investors

Investors are increasingly looking at non-financial factors when deciding where to put their money. Ethical leadership, particularly in areas like ESG (Environmental, Social, and Governance), is a key criterion for investors. A company that demonstrates a commitment to ethical practices and sustainability is likely to attract long-term investors who value integrity and social responsibility.

How to Develop Ethical Leadership Skills

Becoming an ethical leader requires intentional effort. It's not just about following the rules but about modelling the behaviors you want to see in your organization. Here are some ways to develop and strengthen your ethical leadership skills:

1. Lead by Example

As CEO, your behavior sets the standard for the entire organization. If you want to build an ethical culture, you must embody the values you promote. This means making tough decisions that align with your company's values—even when those decisions are not the easiest or most profitable in the short term. Demonstrate honesty, transparency, and accountability in every aspect of your leadership.

2. Prioritize Integrity in Decision-Making

Integrity is the cornerstone of ethical leadership. When faced with difficult choices, always ask yourself: **"What is the right thing to do?"** Ethical decisions may not always align with the most convenient option, but they will strengthen your company's reputation and ensure long-term sustainability. By prioritizing integrity in your decision-making, you set a standard for others to follow.

3. Foster a Culture of Open Communication

Create an environment where employees feel safe to speak up about ethical concerns, report misconduct, or offer feedback. Ethical leaders encourage transparency and open dialogue, which helps identify and address potential issues before they escalate. An anonymous whistleblower system can also help protect employees who need to report unethical behavior.

4. Implement Diversity, Equity, and Inclusion (DEI) Initiatives

Ethical leadership means ensuring that everyone within your organization has equal opportunities, regardless of their background, identity, or gender. Prioritize DEI by promoting an inclusive workplace where diverse perspectives are valued and individuals are treated fairly. Establish clear policies for addressing discrimination and bias.

5. Integrate ESG (Environmental, Social, and Governance) Principles

Ethical leadership extends beyond the confines of the office—it involves a commitment to social and environmental responsibility. CEOs must champion **ESG** initiatives that address environmental sustainability, social justice, and good governance. This includes responsible sourcing, reducing the company's carbon footprint, supporting local communities, and maintaining high standards of corporate governance.

6. Continuous Learning and Reflection

Ethical leadership is not a destination; it's a journey. Continuously reflect on your decisions and actions. Seek feedback from colleagues, mentors, and stakeholders. Participate in leadership development programs, workshops, or courses on ethics, DEI, and ESG. Stay informed about best practices and emerging trends in ethical leadership.

Tools for Ethical Leadership

Several tools and frameworks can help guide your ethical leadership journey:

- **Code of Ethics**: A clearly articulated **Code of Ethics** sets the expectations for behavior within your company. It provides a framework for making ethical decisions and helps employees understand the company's values.

- **Ethics Training**: Regular ethics training programs for employees ensure that everyone understands the company's ethical guidelines and how to apply them in their day-to-day work.

- **DEI and ESG Metrics**: Set specific metrics for measuring progress in areas such as diversity, equity, and inclusion, as well as environmental sustainability and governance. These metrics will help track the effectiveness of your ethical leadership practices and hold you accountable.

- **Whistleblower Protection Systems**: Ensure that there are clear channels for employees to report unethical behavior without fear of retaliation.

Practical Steps to Implement Ethical Leadership Principles

Here are practical steps you can take to strengthen your ethical leadership principles:

1. **Define Your Core Values**: Reflect on your personal values and the ethical principles you want to guide your leadership. Write them down and share them with your team. These values should align with the mission and vision of the company.

2. **Establish Clear Expectations**: Make sure that everyone in your organization understands what is expected of them in terms of ethical behavior. Create policies, training programs, and performance metrics that reinforce these expectations.

3. **Promote Accountability**: Hold yourself and others accountable for ethical behavior. Implement regular reviews, audits, and performance assessments to ensure that your organization is adhering to ethical standards.

4. **Actively Champion DEI and ESG**: Develop and promote initiatives that support diversity, equity, and inclusion, as well as environmental and social responsibility. Set measurable goals for your company's DEI and ESG efforts and regularly report on progress.

5. **Encourage Open Dialogue**: Foster a culture of transparency where employees feel safe raising ethical concerns and suggesting improvements. Regularly engage with your team, listen to their feedback, and address any issues that arise.

6. **Make Ethics Part of Your Brand**: Integrate ethical principles into your company's branding, marketing, and communications. Show the world that your company is committed to ethical practices, and demonstrate how your business decisions reflect this commitment.

Real-Life Case Study: Paul Polman and Unilever's Ethical Leadership

Paul Polman, former CEO of **Unilever**, is a prime example of how ethical leadership can drive business success. When Polman took the helm at Unilever in 2009, he faced a company that was grappling with sustainability issues, a focus on short-term profits, and growing consumer demand for responsible business practices.

Polman's approach was revolutionary. He made the decision to stop providing quarterly earnings reports, shifting the focus from short-term profits to long-term sustainable growth. He also implemented the **Unilever Sustainable Living Plan**, which committed the company to a wide range of environmental and social goals, such as reducing its carbon footprint, improving the health and well-being of millions of people, and promoting sustainable sourcing.

By embracing **ESG** principles and fostering a culture of responsibility and ethical decision-making, Polman led Unilever to not only become a global leader in sustainability but also achieve strong financial performance. Under his leadership, Unilever's stock price increased by over 200%, and the company was consistently ranked among the world's most ethical businesses.

Polman's success demonstrates how ethical leadership can drive both corporate growth and positive social impact. His ability to integrate ethical principles into Unilever's core business strategy helped the company build trust with consumers, employees, and investors, while also achieving significant business results.

Conclusion: Ethical Leadership as the Bedrock of Sustainable Success

Ethical leadership is the cornerstone of trust, loyalty, and long-term success in business. As a CEO, your ability to lead with integrity, prioritize diversity and inclusion, and integrate ESG principles into your business strategy will define the future of your organization. By modelling ethical behavior, setting clear expectations, and fostering a culture of transparency, you can create an organization that not only thrives but also contributes positively to society.

Remember, ethical leadership is not a one-time achievement—it's a continuous journey. By committing to ethical principles every day, you can drive both business success and social good, positioning your company for sustainable growth and creating a lasting legacy.

19

Corporate Governance & Compliance

In today's complex and ever-changing business environment, corporate governance and compliance have never been more important. For a CEO, understanding and implementing strong governance practices is essential not only for mitigating risk but also for ensuring the long-term success and sustainability of the company. Corporate governance serves as the framework for managing an organization's operations, ensuring accountability, fairness, and transparency in its relationships with stakeholders, including shareholders, employees, customers, and the wider community.

In this chapter, we will explore what corporate governance is, how to build a governance and compliance framework, the importance of board reporting, and the tools that can help ensure effective governance. We will also provide practical steps for developing a robust governance and compliance protocol, along with a real-life case study of a CEO who successfully implemented these practices to drive corporate growth and integrity.

What is Corporate Governance?

Corporate governance refers to the systems, principles, and processes by which a company is directed and controlled. It involves establishing policies and practices that ensure the organization operates transparently, ethically, and in alignment with the interests of all stakeholders. Governance is about balancing the needs of the company's shareholders, management, customers, suppliers, and the wider community. A strong governance structure provides clarity on roles, responsibilities, and the decision-making process.

Good corporate governance ensures:

- **Accountability:** Managers and executives are held accountable for their decisions and actions.

- **Transparency:** Decisions, financial reports, and business operations are open and honest.

- **Fairness:** Stakeholders, including employees and customers, are treated equitably.

- **Sustainability:** Governance frameworks promote the long-term growth and sustainability of the company.

- **Ethical Conduct:** The company adheres to high standards of ethical behavior and corporate responsibility.

How to Build a Governance and Compliance Framework

Creating a governance and compliance framework involves developing policies, procedures, and structures that ensure your company meets legal and regulatory requirements, operates ethically, and is prepared to navigate risks. Here's how to develop a robust governance and compliance framework:

1. Define the Governance Structure

A well-defined governance structure is the foundation of effective corporate governance. This includes establishing roles and responsibilities within the company, particularly for the **board of directors**, **executive leadership**, and **management teams**.

- **Board of Directors:** The board is responsible for overseeing management and ensuring that the company adheres to legal and ethical standards. They must be independent, knowledgeable, and engaged in governance matters.

- **CEO and Executive Leadership Team:** The CEO and executives implement the strategies, decisions, and operations aligned with the governance framework. They report to the board and ensure the company's operations are in line with governance protocols.

- **Compliance Officer/Team:** A dedicated compliance officer or team is essential for monitoring adherence to regulatory requirements, industry standards, and ethical guidelines.

2. Establish Policies and Procedures

Create a comprehensive set of policies that outline the company's approach to key areas, such as:

- **Code of Conduct**: Set expectations for ethical behavior at all levels of the organization.

- **Conflict of Interest**: Define what constitutes a conflict of interest and outline the process for disclosure and resolution.

- **Anti-corruption and Anti-bribery Policies**: Implement measures to prevent corruption, bribery, and unethical business practices.

- **Risk Management Policies**: Identify potential risks and outline strategies for mitigating them.

- **Whistleblower Protections**: Establish safe and anonymous channels for employees to report misconduct or unethical behavior.

3. Compliance with Legal and Regulatory Requirements

Ensure your governance framework is aligned with national and international laws and regulations. This includes compliance with:

- **Financial Reporting and Auditing Standards**: Adhere to **GAAP** (Generally Accepted Accounting Principles) or **IFRS** (International Financial Reporting Standards) and ensure accurate financial reporting.

- **Industry-Specific Regulations**: Comply with industry-specific regulations (e.g., healthcare, finance, technology) and certifications (e.g., HIPAA, GDPR).

- **Tax and Employment Laws**: Stay compliant with tax laws, labor laws, and other relevant regulations in your jurisdiction.

4. Establish Clear Communication Channels

Transparent communication is critical for good governance. Establish clear channels between the board, executive leadership, and employees. Regular reporting, updates, and meetings with the board help ensure that governance decisions align with the organization's goals and that potential issues are identified early.

5. Monitor and Evaluate Governance and Compliance

Regularly monitor the effectiveness of your governance framework through internal audits, compliance reviews, and board assessments. Ensure that the company is adhering to its policies, identifying areas for improvement, and addressing emerging risks. This includes:

- **Internal Audits**: Regular audits of financial and operational processes help identify and mitigate potential risks.

- **Compliance Training**: Provide ongoing training to employees on compliance standards, ethical behavior, and regulatory requirements.

- **Feedback Loops**: Gather feedback from employees and stakeholders to continually improve governance practices.

Board Reporting for Governance

One of the most critical aspects of corporate governance is the **board reporting process**. The board of directors relies on accurate, transparent, and timely information to make informed decisions and ensure that the company's management is adhering to governance and compliance practices.

Effective board reporting should include:

- **Financial Performance Reports**: Clear, detailed reports on the company's financial health, including revenue, expenses, profits, and liabilities.

- **Risk Reports**: An analysis of potential risks facing the company, along with strategies for mitigating them.

- **Compliance Updates**: Regular updates on the company's adherence to legal and regulatory requirements.

- **Ethical Compliance and Whistleblower Reports**: A summary of ethical practices, including any whistleblower reports, investigations, or concerns.

- **Strategic Plans**: Updates on the company's long-term strategy and how governance aligns with corporate objectives.

Tools for Governance and Compliance

To build a robust governance and compliance system, CEOs can leverage various tools and technologies that streamline processes, improve efficiency, and ensure transparency. These tools include:

- **Governance, Risk, and Compliance (GRC) Software**: These tools help manage and monitor governance, risk, and compliance processes, track performance, and ensure that standards are met. Examples include **LogicManager** and **Diligent**.

- **Internal Auditing Software**: Automate internal auditing processes with software such as **AuditBoard** to assess financial and operational risk and maintain compliance.

- **Compliance Management Systems (CMS)**: Use CMS tools like **ComplyAdvantage** or **Convercent** to track legal and regulatory requirements, manage compliance tasks, and document adherence.

- **Whistleblower Reporting Systems**: Implement anonymous reporting systems through third-party services such as **EthicsPoint** to encourage employees to report unethical behavior safely.

Practical Steps to Develop Corporate Governance and Compliance Protocols

1. **Assess Current Governance Structure**: Evaluate the current governance structure to ensure that roles and responsibilities are clear, the board is independent, and key compliance functions are in place.

2. **Develop or Update Key Policies**: Ensure that you have a comprehensive set of policies covering ethics, risk management, conflict of interest, anti-corruption, and more. Regularly update these to stay compliant with changing regulations.

3. **Implement a Compliance Training Program**: Conduct regular training for all employees, particularly senior leaders and board members, on governance policies, regulatory requirements, and ethical conduct.

4. **Establish a Risk Management Framework**: Identify key risks to your organization, such as financial, operational, or reputational risks, and develop a framework to mitigate these risks. This should be a continuous process of monitoring, evaluation, and adjustment.

5. **Strengthen Board Reporting**: Implement clear and consistent board reporting systems that ensure the board receives accurate, timely, and relevant information to make informed decisions.

6. **Use Technology**: Invest in governance, risk, and compliance (GRC) software to streamline governance processes and ensure accountability. These tools will help you track compliance, manage risks, and maintain proper documentation.

7. **Encourage Open Communication and Transparency**: Foster an open culture where governance and compliance are seen as everyone's responsibility, and where employees feel empowered to report concerns without fear of retaliation.

Case Study: Howard Schultz and Starbucks' Corporate Governance Success

Howard Schultz, the former CEO of Starbucks, provides a compelling example of how strong corporate governance and compliance can drive business success. When Schultz took over Starbucks in the early 1980s, he was faced with the challenge of scaling a rapidly growing company while maintaining ethical standards and sound governance practices.

Schultz's commitment to **corporate responsibility**, **employee welfare**, and **community engagement** became core tenets of Starbucks' corporate governance framework. He established clear governance practices that included a strong **board of directors** overseeing corporate decisions, a transparent **code of conduct** for employees, and a commitment to **social responsibility**. He was a champion of diversity, equity, and inclusion (DEI), long before these became industry buzzwords.

Starbucks also became known for its commitment to **ESG** principles, integrating environmental sustainability and social impact into the company's business strategy. Schultz's leadership ensured that Starbucks adhered to high standards of corporate governance, which allowed the company to scale rapidly while maintaining its reputation for ethical behavior and corporate responsibility.

Under Schultz's leadership, Starbucks grew from a small regional coffee shop to a global brand, generating billions in revenue and creating a highly engaged and loyal customer base. His emphasis on corporate governance and compliance was instrumental in building trust with consumers, employees, and investors, making Starbucks a model for other companies to follow.

Conclusion: Corporate Governance and Compliance as a Cornerstone of Leadership

Effective corporate governance and compliance are critical for any CEO who wants to lead a successful and sustainable company. By implementing a robust governance framework, prioritizing transparency, and fostering ethical decision-making, you can create a company that thrives in both performance and reputation. The steps outlined in this chapter, combined with the tools and practices shared, will help you build a governance and compliance program that ensures accountability, promotes trust, and drives long-term success.

Remember, the decisions you make as a CEO have far-reaching consequences. Ethical leadership, sound governance, and compliance are not optional—they are essential to achieving business success, gaining stakeholder trust, and positioning your company for sustainable growth in the years to come.

20

Technology and Artificial Intelligence

In the rapidly evolving world of business, technology plays a pivotal role in driving growth, improving efficiency, and enhancing competitive advantage. For a CEO, understanding how technology can optimize operations, streamline workflows, and support strategic goals is essential. In this chapter, we will explore how technology can transform business operations, how to build a high-performance technology team, the role of artificial intelligence (AI) and robotic process automation (RPA), and how to develop technology programs that directly add value to the organization.

We will also provide actionable steps you can take to develop a robust technology division within your company and offer a real-life case study illustrating how one CEO successfully built a strong technology division to drive innovation and growth.

What Technology Can Do to Facilitate Business Operations

Technology is no longer a luxury; it's a necessity for companies seeking to stay competitive and efficient. Here's how technology can transform your business:

1. Automation of Repetitive Tasks:

Technology can automate repetitive and time-consuming tasks, allowing employees to focus on more strategic work. Tools like **Robotic Process Automation (RPA)** can handle everything from data entry to invoice processing, freeing up valuable human resources.

2. Data-Driven Decision Making:

Advanced analytics and business intelligence tools enable companies to collect and analyze data in real-time. This data-driven approach allows CEOs and executives to make informed decisions that are based on facts, not just intuition.

3. Streamlining Communication and Collaboration:

Modern communication tools like **Slack, Microsoft Teams**, and **Zoom** facilitate collaboration across departments and geographic locations. This results in quicker decision-making and enhances team cohesion.

4. Enhancing Customer Experience:

Technology enables companies to personalize customer interactions through data insights. CRM (Customer Relationship Management) systems, powered by AI, can provide tailored experiences and improve customer retention.

5. Optimizing Supply Chain and Operations:

Technology allows businesses to manage and monitor their supply chains with precision. Using platforms like **SAP** or **Oracle**, companies can track inventory, forecast demand, and optimize production schedules to reduce costs and improve efficiency.

6. Security and Compliance:

As businesses increasingly rely on technology, ensuring cybersecurity and compliance with data privacy regulations is vital. Tools like **firewalls, encryption**, and compliance management software protect sensitive data and safeguard against potential threats.

Building a Coherent Technology Division

To leverage technology effectively, the CEO must prioritize building a **coherent technology division** that aligns with the company's overall strategy and objectives. Here's how to do that:

1. Understand the Technology Needs of Your Business:

Before building a technology division, understand your company's goals and challenges. Technology should not be seen as an isolated function but as an enabler of business strategy. Are you aiming for faster growth? Improved customer experience? Operational efficiency? Identifying these goals will help shape the technology vision.

2. Recruit and Build the Right Talent:

Building a high-performance technology team starts with hiring the right people. Look for employees with both technical skills and business acumen. A blend of software engineers, data scientists, UX/UI designers, and technology strategists will create a well-rounded team. Furthermore, encourage continuous learning and skill development to keep your team ahead of technological trends.

3. Implement Clear Roles and Responsibilities:

For technology to work effectively within a company, each member of the technology team must have clearly defined roles and responsibilities. Consider the following key roles:

- **Chief Technology Officer (CTO):** The leader of the technology division, responsible for overseeing all technological initiatives and ensuring alignment with business goals.

- **Software Developers:** Engineers who build and maintain the company's digital tools, platforms, and systems.

- **Data Scientists/Analysts:** Specialists in analyzing data to derive insights and inform business strategy.

- **IT Support Specialists:** Experts who maintain the company's infrastructure, ensuring systems run smoothly.

Make sure there's a clear reporting structure, and team members understand their role in the broader mission of the company.

4. Foster Cross-Department Collaboration:

The technology division should not operate in isolation. Collaborating with other departments, such as marketing, operations, and finance, ensures that technology programs are aligned with the needs of the business. Cross-functional teams can share insights, solve problems together, and ensure the technology implementation is smooth.

The Role of Artificial Intelligence (AI) and Robotic Process Automation (RPA) in Modern Companies

Two key technologies that are revolutionizing the business landscape today are **Artificial Intelligence (AI)** and **Robotic Process Automation (RPA)**.

Artificial Intelligence (AI):

AI is transforming how businesses approach data analysis, customer service, and decision-making. AI systems can recognize patterns, predict outcomes, and even automate decision-making processes in some cases. In the context of a CEO, AI can be used to:

- Predict market trends, customer behavior, and operational issues.

- Optimize pricing strategies and product recommendations through machine learning.

- Enhance customer service with chatbots and virtual assistants, providing personalized responses in real-time.

Robotic Process Automation (RPA):

RPA uses software robots or "bots" to automate repetitive, rule-based tasks, such as data entry, invoice generation, and report creation. RPA can significantly reduce operational costs, enhance efficiency, and improve accuracy by eliminating human error. For CEOs, RPA offers the opportunity to:

- Streamline back-office operations.

- Improve workflow efficiency and speed.

- Free up employees to focus on higher-value tasks that require creativity or critical thinking.

When used strategically, both AI and RPA can make a significant impact on operational efficiency, customer satisfaction, and bottom-line performance.

How to Develop Technology Programs that Add Value to Business Operations

To ensure your technology initiatives contribute to your company's success, focus on these key principles:

1. Align Technology with Business Goals:

Technology should be directly tied to your company's strategic objectives. Whether it's driving growth, improving operational efficiency, or enhancing customer experience, every technology initiative should have a clear business outcome.

2. Start Small, Scale Gradually:

Instead of launching large-scale tech initiatives, start with pilot programs. Test new tools or systems in a controlled environment to gauge their effectiveness. Once you have a proven solution, scale it across the organization.

3. Foster a Culture of Innovation:

Encourage your technology team to continuously explore new ideas and experiment with emerging technologies. A culture of innovation leads to greater adaptability and helps the company stay ahead of competitors.

4. Measure Impact and ROI:

Every technology program should be measured for its return on investment (ROI). Utilize performance metrics, KPIs, and data analytics to track how well the technology is delivering on its goals, and adjust your strategies as necessary.

5. Prioritize User Experience:

Technology should not only be functional; it must also be easy to use. Focus on user experience (UX) design and usability. Whether it's your internal systems or customer-facing platforms, intuitive technology can improve both employee productivity and customer satisfaction.

Practical Steps to Develop a Robust Technology Division

1. **Assess Your Current Technology Stack:** Review your existing technology infrastructure and assess whether it's meeting your needs. Are there areas for improvement? Identify gaps and opportunities for growth.

2. **Hire the Right People:** As mentioned earlier, build a team that combines both technical expertise and business insight. Look for candidates who can not only solve technical problems but also understand how their work impacts the broader business.

3. **Create a Technology Roadmap:** Develop a long-term technology strategy that aligns with your business goals. Break this roadmap down into clear, actionable projects that can be executed over time.

4. **Invest in the Right Tools and Platforms:** Choose software and tools that will help improve operations. Evaluate options based on their scalability, ease of use, and integration with your existing systems.

5. **Foster a Continuous Learning Culture:** Encourage ongoing training and professional development. The technology landscape evolves quickly, and it's essential that your team stays up-to-date on the latest advancements.

6. **Measure Success:** Use analytics and performance metrics to track how your technology initiatives are performing. Continuously evaluate and refine your strategy to ensure you are achieving desired outcomes.

Case Study: Satya Nadella and Microsoft's Technology Transformation

Satya Nadella's leadership at **Microsoft** provides an excellent example of how a CEO can build a strong technology division that drives growth and innovation. When Nadella took over as CEO in 2014, Microsoft was a technology giant, but it was facing challenges adapting to cloud computing, mobile technology, and AI.

Nadella recognized the need for a cultural shift within the company. Under his leadership, Microsoft pivoted from a traditional software company to a **cloud-first, mobile-first** business. Nadella focused on building a high-performance technology division centered around **cloud computing**, **artificial intelligence**, and **machine learning**. He emphasized the importance of **cross-team collaboration** and fostered a culture of **innovation** within the company.

Nadella's strategy involved investing heavily in **Azure**, Microsoft's cloud platform, and scaling it to compete with giants like Amazon Web Services (AWS). Additionally, he pushed forward with AI initiatives, integrating machine learning into Microsoft's products like **Office 365** and **LinkedIn**.

The result? Microsoft not only redefined its technological offerings but also achieved remarkable financial success, with **Azure** becoming one of the leading cloud platforms globally. By aligning technology with business strategy and focusing on emerging technologies, Nadella ensured that Microsoft remained a powerhouse in the tech world.

Conclusion: Technology as a Catalyst for Business Success

For a CEO, understanding the importance of technology and how to leverage it for business growth is no longer optional—it's essential. A strong technology division can improve operations, drive innovation, and help the company stay competitive in a fast-paced market. By building a high-performance technology team, embracing AI and RPA, and ensuring that technology programs align with business objectives, you can create a sustainable, tech-forward organization.

In the modern business landscape, the strategic use of technology is the key to achieving not only operational excellence but also long-term success. Whether it's through enhanced efficiency, improved customer experiences, or innovative new products, technology is the foundation for the future of business. As a CEO, it's your responsibility to lead this transformation and unlock the full potential of technology for your organization.

21

The Strengths of Feedback

As a CEO, feedback is one of the most powerful tools in your leadership arsenal. It can drive change, improve performance, and elevate your company to new heights. However, feedback is not just about hearing what's wrong—it's about understanding, reflecting, and taking the right actions to improve. The most successful CEOs view feedback as a vital part of their continuous growth and a crucial mechanism for improving their organization's operations.

In this chapter, we will explore the different types of feedback, why feedback is essential, and how to leverage it to improve corporate performance. We'll also discuss how feedback can shape performance appraisals and training programs. Most importantly, we will cover how to handle feedback constructively, both as a leader and for your team.

By the end of this chapter, you'll have the tools and mindset to turn feedback into a force for improvement within your organization.

The Types of Feedback

Feedback can come in many forms, and understanding these types will help you apply them effectively. Here are the most common types of feedback you'll encounter as a CEO:

1. Constructive Feedback:

This type of feedback is aimed at providing insights on areas of improvement. It's not about pointing out what went wrong but guiding others on how to improve moving forward. Constructive feedback is specific, actionable, and focused on solutions. As a CEO, you must provide this kind of feedback regularly to both your leadership team and staff.

2. Positive Feedback:

This type of feedback focuses on what's going right. It reinforces good behaviors, achievements, and efforts, encouraging people to keep up the good work. As a CEO, offering positive feedback boosts morale and drives employee engagement, making your team feel valued.

3. Peer-to-Peer Feedback:

Feedback doesn't always need to come from the top down. Peer-to-peer feedback encourages team members to offer insights to one another. It fosters a collaborative work environment where individuals learn from each other and grow together.

4. Upward Feedback:

Upward feedback occurs when employees give feedback to their superiors. As a CEO, you should actively encourage this type of feedback. It provides valuable insights into how your leadership style is impacting the team and whether there are any areas that need adjustment.

5. 360-Degree Feedback:

This method of feedback gathers input from various sources—supervisors, peers, and subordinates. 360-degree feedback is a comprehensive approach that offers a balanced perspective on an individual's performance and can be particularly useful during performance appraisals or leadership development programs.

The Importance of Feedback

Feedback is essential because it provides the data you need to assess both personal and organizational performance. Here's why feedback matters:

1. Drives Improvement:

The most immediate and direct benefit of feedback is the ability to drive improvement. By identifying areas for growth, feedback offers you and your team the opportunity to develop new skills, refine strategies, and optimize performance.

2. Enhances Decision-Making:

As a CEO, feedback provides you with the information necessary to make informed decisions. Whether it's market feedback from customers or internal feedback from employees, this data helps you understand what's working and what needs to change.

3. Encourages Continuous Learning:

The best leaders are lifelong learners. Feedback helps you and your team recognize that there is always room for growth. It helps develop a culture of learning and self-improvement, which is crucial for sustaining long-term success.

4. Increases Accountability:

By giving and receiving feedback, you establish a system of accountability throughout the organization. When employees understand that their performance will be reviewed regularly, they are more likely to take ownership of their responsibilities and strive for excellence.

5. Strengthens Relationships:

Feedback is a powerful tool for building trust and improving relationships. When done right, it shows your team that you care about their growth and are invested in their success. It creates an open communication channel, leading to stronger working relationships and greater collaboration.

Feedback's Role in Performance Appraisals and Training Programs

Feedback plays a central role in performance appraisals and the development of training programs. Here's how it works:

1. Performance Appraisals:

Feedback is the cornerstone of performance evaluations. Regular feedback allows employees to understand how they're performing, where they excel, and where they need to improve. As a CEO, make sure that performance appraisals are built around clear, measurable metrics, and use both positive and constructive feedback to guide the conversation.

Tip:

Use a balanced feedback approach that addresses both strengths and areas for growth. Focus on specific actions, not personality traits.

2. Identifying Training Needs:

Feedback often reveals knowledge gaps or skills that employees need to develop. By closely analyzing feedback, you can identify training needs and design programs that address those gaps. For example, if multiple employees are struggling with a particular software tool, it might indicate the need for a company-wide training session.

How Feedback Drives Improved Corporate Operations

When CEOs effectively leverage feedback, it leads to more efficient operations across the organization. Here's how:

1. Streamlining Processes:

Feedback from employees at all levels can help identify inefficiencies and bottlenecks in operations. By listening to feedback on internal processes, you can make changes to streamline workflows and reduce redundancy.

2. Improving Customer Satisfaction:

Customer feedback, whether through surveys, reviews, or direct communication, can offer valuable insights into how your products or services are meeting market needs. As a CEO, responding to customer feedback and implementing changes based on it can lead to higher customer satisfaction and retention.

3. Enhancing Company Culture:

Employee feedback helps shape company culture. If employees are regularly asked for their opinions and feel heard, they are more likely to be engaged and motivated. A healthy feedback culture fosters transparency, trust, and collaboration.

4. Driving Innovation:

Feedback from both customers and employees can spark new ideas and innovations. Listening to what people need and want, and acting on that feedback, helps your company stay ahead of the competition.

Taking the Right Attitude Toward Feedback

To make the most out of feedback, it's crucial to approach it with the right mindset. Here's how to handle feedback constructively:

1. Be Open-Minded:

Approach feedback with curiosity, not defensiveness. Remember that feedback is a gift, even when it's difficult to hear. Be willing to listen and absorb it without getting emotional or defensive.

2. Separate Ego from Feedback:

Feedback is about performance, not your personal worth. Don't let negative feedback undermine your self-esteem. See it as an opportunity to learn and grow.

3. Act on Feedback:

Feedback is only valuable if it leads to action. Don't just listen—implement changes based on the feedback you receive. Whether it's improving your leadership style or refining an operational process, make adjustments and communicate those changes to your team.

4. Provide Constructive Feedback to Others:

As a CEO, you are also responsible for providing feedback to your team. Make sure that your feedback is constructive, actionable, and delivered in a way that fosters growth. Avoid blame and focus on solutions.

Practical Steps to Handle Feedback Constructively

1. **Listen Actively:** When receiving feedback, listen without interrupting. Let the person speak fully before you respond, and ask clarifying questions if needed.

2. **Acknowledge the Feedback:** Show appreciation for the feedback, even if it's critical. A simple "Thank you for sharing this with me" can go a long way in building trust.

3. **Reflect and Evaluate:** Take time to reflect on the feedback you receive. Evaluate whether the points raised are valid and think about how you can improve.

4. **Take Action:** Develop a plan to act on the feedback. Whether it's through small adjustments or significant changes, taking action is the key to improvement.

5. **Follow Up:** After implementing changes, check back in with the person who provided the feedback to see if the issue has been resolved or if further improvement is needed.

Case Study: Jeff Bezos and Amazon's Feedback-Driven Culture

One of the most well-known examples of a CEO leveraging feedback to achieve better performance is Jeff Bezos, the founder and former CEO of Amazon. From the early days of Amazon, Bezos prioritized a **customer-centric feedback culture**, where feedback from customers and employees alike was not only welcomed but actively sought out.

Bezos used customer feedback to refine and optimize Amazon's offerings, constantly adjusting the company's products, services, and even its core business model. For example, the introduction of Amazon Prime was heavily influenced by feedback from loyal customers who desired faster shipping options. In turn, Bezos cultivated a culture where employees were encouraged to give and receive feedback constantly, fostering innovation and operational efficiency.

Moreover, Amazon's internal feedback systems allowed employees to constantly improve processes, leading to a dramatic reduction in inefficiencies. As a result, Amazon grew from an online bookstore into one of the world's largest and most successful tech companies.

Conclusion

Feedback is a powerful tool that drives improvement, fosters innovation, and enhances performance. As a CEO, it is critical to foster a feedback culture within your organization. Whether it's providing constructive feedback to your team, receiving feedback from employees, or listening to customer feedback, the insights you gain can help shape the future of your business.

By taking a constructive attitude toward feedback, using it to guide performance appraisals and training programs, and implementing changes based on it, you can ensure continuous growth and operational excellence. Embrace feedback, and turn it into a catalyst for success in your leadership journey.

22

The Importance of Gratitude

Gratitude is often seen as a soft skill, something that's nice to practice but not essential in the high-stakes world of corporate leadership. However, the truth is that gratitude is one of the most powerful tools a CEO can use to inspire their teams, create a positive corporate culture, and drive company success.

In this chapter, we'll explore why gratitude is so important for a CEO, how it can be harnessed to improve team performance and morale, and the steps you can take to develop and foster a culture of gratitude within your company.

The Importance of Gratitude in Leadership

Gratitude is not just about saying "thank you" when someone does something good for you. It's about recognizing the effort, contributions, and successes of others—whether it's your team, your clients, or even yourself. For a CEO, embracing gratitude in leadership can have profound effects on organizational success.

1. Fosters a Positive Corporate Culture:

Gratitude is at the heart of any healthy organizational culture. When leaders express appreciation for their teams' hard work, it creates an environment of trust, respect, and mutual support. Employees feel valued, which makes them more motivated, engaged, and loyal to the company.

2. Drives Employee Engagement and Motivation:

Employees who feel appreciated are more likely to go above and beyond. Gratitude from leadership provides the positive reinforcement that employees need to continue performing at their best. It helps them feel seen and heard, driving a sense of ownership and pride in their work.

3. Builds Stronger Relationships:

A culture of gratitude doesn't just benefit your team—it strengthens relationships between leadership, employees, and clients. When you regularly express gratitude, you build stronger connections based on respect and appreciation. This can lead to better collaboration, a more cohesive team, and stronger external relationships.

4. Increases Retention and Decreases Turnover:

High turnover can be costly, both in terms of time and money. When a CEO regularly practices gratitude, it leads to a happier, more satisfied workforce. Employees are more likely to stay in a company that values their contributions, which improves retention and reduces the costs associated with recruitment and training.

Things to Be Grateful For as a CEO

As a CEO, it's easy to get caught up in the challenges and demands of the role. But it's crucial to take a step back and reflect on the many things you should be grateful for:

1. Your Team:

Your employees are the driving force behind your company's success. Be grateful for their talent, dedication, and hard work. Acknowledge the contributions of individuals and teams alike, and show appreciation for their role in achieving business objectives.

2. Your Clients and Customers:

Without clients, there would be no business. Be grateful for the relationships you have with customers, clients, and partners. Their trust in your products or services is invaluable and key to your company's growth.

3. Opportunities for Growth:

As a CEO, you have a unique perspective on the potential your company has. Be grateful for the opportunity to lead, innovate, and make decisions that shape the future of the organization. Embrace the challenges as opportunities for growth.

4. The Support of Your Leadership Team:

A CEO is not an island. Your leadership team plays a crucial role in helping you execute the company's vision. Show gratitude for their support, commitment, and ability to tackle complex challenges alongside you.

5. Business Milestones and Achievements:

Take time to recognize the wins, both big and small. Every milestone, whether it's launching a new product or hitting a sales target, is a result of collective effort. Celebrate these achievements with gratitude and reflect on how they came about.

Fostering a Culture of Gratitude in Your Company

As a CEO, your actions set the tone for the entire organization. When you express gratitude, it encourages others to do the same. Fostering a culture of gratitude within your company can yield impressive results, including improved team morale, productivity, and job satisfaction.

Here's how you can create a gratitude-driven culture:

1. Lead by Example:

The best way to instill a culture of gratitude is by practicing it yourself. Make it a habit to regularly thank your employees, whether through personal recognition or in public settings. When you make gratitude a part of your leadership style, your team will follow suit.

2. Praise and Recognition:

Don't wait for annual performance reviews to offer praise. Offer regular and specific recognition when employees do something well. Whether it's acknowledging a team's successful project or recognizing an individual's contribution to a key milestone, appreciation should be ongoing.

Tip:

Start team meetings with recognition—highlight individual or team achievements and publicly thank those who have made an impact.

3. Create Structured Recognition Programs:

While informal gratitude is powerful, structured recognition programs can further enhance a gratitude-driven culture. Consider establishing awards or recognition platforms, such as "Employee of the Month" or peer-nominated acknowledgments, to show appreciation for outstanding contributions.

4. Encourage Peer-to-Peer Gratitude:

Gratitude shouldn't just flow from the top down. Encourage your employees to express gratitude to one another. This builds camaraderie and reinforces a positive, supportive environment throughout the organization. Peer recognition programs can be an effective way to foster this.

5. Give Credit Where It's Due:

Acknowledge the efforts and successes of your team at every opportunity. When talking about your company's achievements, always give credit to the team behind it. Recognizing others' contributions in public spaces—whether in meetings, emails, or company newsletters—creates a culture where employees feel valued.

Practical Steps to Build a Positive and Grateful Attitude

Developing a habit of gratitude requires conscious effort, but with the following steps, you can transform your leadership style and your company's culture:

1. Start Your Day with Gratitude:

Begin each day by reflecting on what you are grateful for—whether it's the opportunity to lead, the progress your company is making, or the team you work with. Taking a few moments each morning to express gratitude can set a positive tone for the rest of the day.

2. Practice Active Listening:

When employees share their thoughts or feedback, listen actively and acknowledge their contributions. Showing appreciation for their input builds trust and makes them feel heard.

3. Write Thank-You Notes:

A handwritten note or a personalized email can go a long way in expressing gratitude. Take the time to write thank-you notes to employees, clients, or partners who have gone above and beyond. This simple act shows that you value their efforts.

4. Regularly Acknowledge Successes:

Make it a practice to recognize both individual and team achievements, whether in a meeting or through company-wide emails. Acknowledging hard work not only shows gratitude but also motivates others to excel.

5. Reflect on Your Leadership Journey:

Take time each week or month to reflect on your leadership journey. Think about the people who have helped you grow and how their contributions have shaped your success. This reflection will keep you grounded and focused on the bigger picture.

Case Study: Howard Schultz and Starbucks: Building a Gratitude-Driven Culture

Howard Schultz, the former CEO of Starbucks, is a prime example of how gratitude can be leveraged to build a positive corporate culture and drive success. Schultz built Starbucks into one of the most successful brands in the world, but a core part of his leadership philosophy was centered around gratitude and recognition.

Schultz often spoke about the importance of treating employees (whom he referred to as "partners") with respect and appreciation. From the very beginning, Schultz made sure that Starbucks' employees received health benefits and stock options, something uncommon in the retail industry at the time. This move was based on his belief that when employees feel valued, they are more likely to provide excellent customer service.

In addition, Schultz was known for regularly visiting Starbucks locations, interacting with employees, and showing genuine gratitude for their hard work. He didn't just thank his top executives—he expressed his gratitude to the baristas and store managers who were on the front lines. This personal recognition played a significant role in fostering a strong sense of loyalty and commitment within the Starbucks team.

As a result of Schultz's focus on gratitude, Starbucks developed a culture where employees were motivated to provide exceptional service, creating a loyal customer base and driving growth. Schultz's leadership showed that gratitude isn't just a feel-good practice—it's a powerful strategy that can lead to business success.

Conclusion

Gratitude is one of the most powerful, yet underutilized, tools in a CEO's leadership toolkit. When practiced consistently, gratitude fosters a positive corporate culture, drives employee motivation, and improves company performance. As a CEO, your ability to recognize and appreciate the efforts of your team can create a ripple effect that strengthens your company and propels it to new heights.

By leading with gratitude, expressing thanks regularly, and building a culture of recognition, you can enhance team morale, boost productivity, and ultimately drive corporate success. The best CEOs know that it's not just about making tough decisions—it's also about showing appreciation for the people who make those decisions possible.

So, start today. Express your gratitude, cultivate a culture of appreciation, and watch your company thrive.

23

Personal Lifestyle Habits

As a CEO, the pressure to lead, perform, and meet expectations can often feel overwhelming. The demands of the role require long hours, strategic decision-making, and constant attention to the business. But amidst these challenges, there is one critical factor that cannot be overlooked: your personal lifestyle. Achieving a balance between work and life, maintaining your health, and fostering happiness and joy is not just important for your well-being—it's essential for your success as a leader.

This chapter will explore how cultivating a healthy personal lifestyle can enhance your leadership abilities. We'll discuss the importance of work-life balance, maintaining good health, pursuing hobbies and interests, protecting mental health, and nurturing relationships. Additionally, we'll provide actionable steps you can take to integrate these principles into your life for better leadership and personal fulfilment.

The Importance of Work-Life Balance

For many CEOs, the idea of work-life balance might seem unrealistic. However, achieving balance isn't about equal time distribution; it's about finding harmony between your professional and personal life. A balanced life leads to greater productivity, better decision-making, and enhanced creativity—qualities that are vital for leadership.

Why Work-Life Balance Matters:

1. **Prevents Burnout:** As a CEO, you are at the center of your company's success. Without balance, you risk burnout, which can reduce your effectiveness and strain your relationships. Taking time to recharge is crucial.

2. **Increases Productivity:** Working non-stop can lead to diminishing returns. By taking regular breaks and ensuring you disconnect from work when necessary, you'll be more focused and efficient when you return to your responsibilities.

3. **Boosts Creativity:** Stepping away from work allows you to gain fresh perspectives. It's when you're not thinking about the business that your best ideas often emerge.

4. **Fosters Resilience:** A healthy work-life balance allows you to build resilience. You're better equipped to handle business challenges with a clear, calm mind.

Building Happiness and Joy

Success is not just about professional milestones; it's about finding fulfilment in all aspects of your life. Happiness and joy don't come automatically—they must be cultivated intentionally. As a CEO, it's easy to focus entirely on work, but nurturing your personal happiness is equally important.

Why Happiness and Joy Matter:

1. **Improves Leadership Quality:** Happy CEOs are more empathetic, approachable, and energized. When you feel joy in your personal life, you bring that positive energy to your professional life.

2. **Enhances Team Morale:** A CEO who exhibits joy and positivity creates a ripple effect throughout the organization. Happy leaders inspire and motivate their teams to perform at their best.

3. **Increases Long-Term Satisfaction:** At the end of your career, it's not just the achievements you'll remember—it's the moments of joy and fulfilment in your life. Building a life you love ensures long-term satisfaction, both personally and professionally.

Maintaining Great Health

As a CEO, your physical health is a foundation for everything else you do. A healthy body supports a sharp mind and the energy needed to lead effectively. It's tempting to neglect health when work demands are high, but taking care of yourself should always be a priority.

How Health Impacts Leadership:

1. **Increases Energy Levels:** Regular exercise and proper nutrition help maintain energy levels, ensuring you can handle the demands of your day.

2. **Sharpens Mental Clarity:** Physical health is directly linked to mental clarity and decision-making. When your body feels good, your mind is more focused and capable of making high-stakes decisions.

3. **Reduces Stress:** Regular physical activity is one of the best ways to reduce stress and prevent the mental and physical toll of a high-pressure job.

Eating Well

The food you consume directly affects your energy levels, mood, and cognitive performance. CEOs must prioritize proper nutrition to sustain peak performance throughout the day.

Healthy Eating Habits:

1. **Prioritize Whole Foods:** Focus on a balanced diet rich in fruits, vegetables, lean proteins, and healthy fats. Minimize processed foods and excessive sugar, which can lead to energy crashes.

2. **Hydrate:** Drink plenty of water throughout the day. Dehydration can lead to fatigue, brain fog, and decreased concentration.

3. **Meal Prep:** Make time to plan and prepare your meals for the week. This will help you avoid unhealthy choices during hectic workdays.

4. **Mindful Eating:** Practice mindful eating by slowing down and focusing on your food. This can help with digestion and prevent overeating.

Taking Time for Exercise

Exercise isn't just for staying in shape—it's a powerful tool for improving mental clarity, reducing stress, and increasing your overall well-being. For a busy CEO, finding time to work out can seem difficult, but the benefits far outweigh the time commitment.

How Exercise Supports Leadership:

1. **Boosts Cognitive Function:** Physical activity increases blood flow to the brain, which can improve focus, memory, and decision-making.

2. **Reduces Stress:** Exercise triggers the release of endorphins, natural mood elevators that help you manage stress and anxiety.

3. **Promotes Longevity:** Maintaining an active lifestyle contributes to overall health, which helps ensure that you can perform at your best throughout your career and beyond.

Pursuing Hobbies and Interests

Your work as a CEO is demanding, but it should not be your only source of fulfilment. Engaging in hobbies and activities outside of your professional life provides an opportunity to recharge and reconnect with your passions.

Why Hobbies Matter:

1. **Promotes Creativity:** Hobbies often involve creative thinking, which can help you approach business challenges with fresh ideas.

2. **Provides a Sense of Achievement:** Whether it's painting, playing a musical instrument, or gardening, hobbies give you a sense of accomplishment outside of your work.

3. **Boosts Well-Being:** Pursuing your interests can reduce stress and increase happiness, which in turn helps you maintain your leadership effectiveness.

Protecting Your Mental Health

Mental health is often the most overlooked aspect of leadership, but it is crucial for long-term success. A CEO who neglects their mental well-being risks burnout, poor decision-making, and strained relationships.

How to Protect Your Mental Health:

1. **Prioritize Self-Care:** Make self-care a priority by incorporating stress-reducing activities like meditation, journaling, or spending time in nature.

2. **Set Boundaries:** Establish clear boundaries between work and personal time. This allows you to fully recharge and prevent work from overwhelming your personal life.

3. **Seek Support:** Don't hesitate to seek professional help if you're feeling overwhelmed. A therapist or coach can provide valuable tools for managing stress and improving mental health.

Maintaining Healthy Relationships with Family and Friends

Your personal relationships are the foundation of your support system. As a CEO, maintaining strong, healthy relationships with friends, family, and loved ones is essential for both personal and professional success.

Why Relationships Matter:

1. **Provide Emotional Support:** Your loved ones provide the emotional support you need to navigate the challenges of leadership. They help you stay grounded and offer perspective when you need it most.

2. **Reduce Stress:** Positive relationships with family and friends help reduce stress and provide an outlet for relaxation and enjoyment.

3. **Encourage Balance:** Healthy relationships encourage work-life balance, reminding you that life is not just about work, but also about connecting with others.

Practical Steps to Build and Integrate a Healthy Personal Lifestyle

Here are some practical steps you can take to create and maintain a personal lifestyle that supports your leadership role:

1. **Set Clear Boundaries:** Define when your workday starts and ends. Use this time to rest, engage with family, or pursue hobbies.

2. **Schedule Time for Exercise:** Treat exercise as a non-negotiable meeting. Block off time in your calendar for physical activity, whether it's a morning run or a yoga session in the evening.

3. **Practice Gratitude:** Start each day by writing down three things you're grateful for. This helps shift your mindset toward positivity and joy.

4. **Plan Healthy Meals:** Create a weekly meal plan that focuses on nutritious, whole foods. This will save you time and ensure you're fueling your body properly.

5. **Engage in Hobbies:** Make time for activities that bring you joy. Whether it's reading, painting, or playing sports, pursuing your passions will help you maintain a healthy work-life balance.

6. **Seek Mental Health Support:** If stress is becoming overwhelming, consider working with a coach or therapist. They can provide strategies to manage pressure and improve your mental well-being.

Case Study: Richard Branson and the Power of a Healthy Lifestyle

Richard Branson, founder of the Virgin Group, is a prime example of a CEO who prioritizes his personal lifestyle to enhance his professional success. Branson is known for his dedication to fitness, adventure, and maintaining a healthy work-life balance.

Despite managing a global empire, Branson has consistently emphasized the importance of exercise, exploration, and mental well-being. He starts his day with a workout, whether it's a swim, a bike ride, or a hike. Branson also dedicates time to pursue his hobbies, such as kite-surfing, and makes it a point to spend quality time with his family.

Branson credits his active lifestyle with keeping his energy levels high and enabling him to stay sharp in his business decisions. By fostering a culture of health, happiness, and gratitude in his personal life, Branson has not only achieved success but also maintained a sense of joy and fulfilment that drives his leadership.

Conclusion

Your personal lifestyle plays a significant role in your success as a CEO. A healthy body, mind, and relationships are essential for effective leadership. By prioritizing work-life balance, health, happiness, and personal fulfilment, you'll be able to lead with greater clarity, energy, and resilience. Take steps today to integrate these principles into your life, and you'll not only become a better CEO—you'll become a better version of yourself.

24

The Pursuit of Excellence

The pursuit of excellence is a core principle that separates great CEOs from the rest. It is not just about meeting expectations; it's about continuously striving to exceed them, in both personal performance and company results. Excellence is not an end destination but an ongoing journey—one that shapes leadership, inspires teams, and drives the long-term success of a business.

In this chapter, we will explore what the pursuit of excellence means for a CEO, how you can set smart goals, hold yourself accountable, build a culture of excellence within your company, and define what success truly looks like. Additionally, we will outline practical steps for you to pursue excellence in both your personal and professional life. Finally, we'll look at a real-life case study of a CEO who embodied the pursuit of excellence to achieve exceptional business growth and leadership development.

What the Pursuit of Excellence Means

The pursuit of excellence is the relentless commitment to improving yourself and your business, regardless of past successes or challenges. It is about striving for the highest standards in everything you do, from the decisions you make to the relationships you build. Excellence is never static; it's a mindset that propels a CEO and their organization forward.

Key Aspects of Pursuing Excellence:

1. **Continuous Improvement:** Excellence requires a commitment to growth. It's not about being perfect, but about always seeking ways to improve your leadership skills, business strategies, and operations.

2. **High Standards:** Setting the bar high for yourself and your company ensures that you are always aiming to deliver quality and achieve outstanding results.

3. **Resilience and Adaptability:** The pursuit of excellence means being prepared to face challenges, learn from failures, and adapt in order to keep moving toward your goals.

4. **Self-Motivation:** Excellence comes from within. You must drive yourself and your team to consistently perform at your best.

Setting SMART Goals for Excellence

Setting clear, achievable goals is a fundamental part of the pursuit of excellence. SMART goals—specific, measurable, achievable, relevant, and time-bound—provide the framework to translate your ambitions into actionable objectives. Without SMART goals, excellence can feel elusive and difficult to attain.

How to Set SMART Goals:

1. **Specific:** Define exactly what you want to achieve. Avoid vague goals like "improve performance." Instead, focus on something precise, such as "increase quarterly revenue by 15%."

2. **Measurable:** Quantify your goals so you can track your progress. For example, "reduce customer service response time to under 24 hours" provides a clear metric.

3. **Achievable:** While goals should be ambitious, they must also be realistic. Ensure that your goals can be accomplished within the given time frame with the resources available.

4. **Relevant:** Ensure your goals align with the company's strategic vision and mission. A goal should be meaningful to the overall direction of the business.

5. **Time-bound:** Set deadlines for each goal. This creates a sense of urgency and helps you focus on meeting milestones along the way.

Example:

- **Goal:** Increase customer retention by 20% within the next 12 months by improving customer experience and providing personalized support.

- **SMART Breakdown:**

  o Specific: Increase customer retention

  o Measurable: By 20%

  o Achievable: With improved customer service initiatives

  o Relevant: Aligns with the company's goal to build a loyal customer base

  o Time-bound: Within 12 months

Holding Yourself Accountable for Excellence

A key trait of successful CEOs is their ability to hold themselves accountable. Accountability drives results and ensures that you stay focused on achieving the goals you've set. This doesn't mean you can't delegate or rely on others—effective leadership is about setting the example and taking responsibility for both successes and failures.

How to Hold Yourself Accountable:

1. **Track Progress Regularly:** Set up regular check-ins with yourself to assess whether you're meeting your goals. This helps you stay focused and makes it easier to course-correct if needed.

2. **Reflect on Mistakes:** When things don't go as planned, don't shy away from taking responsibility. Analyze what went wrong, learn from it, and use it as a stepping stone to improve.

3. **Be Transparent with Your Team:** Lead by example. When you hold yourself accountable, your team will follow suit. Share your goals with them,

and ask for feedback on your performance. Transparency builds trust and motivates your team to strive for excellence as well.

4. **Use a Mentor or Coach:** Sometimes, an external perspective can help hold you accountable. A mentor or executive coach can provide valuable insights, guide your development, and keep you on track.

Building a Culture of Excellence in Your Company

As a CEO, you set the tone for your company's culture. If you're striving for excellence, your team needs to be on board. It's not enough to talk about excellence—you must create an environment where excellence is encouraged, celebrated, and expected.

Key Strategies for Building a Culture of Excellence:

1. **Lead by Example:** Model the behavior you want to see in your team. If you hold yourself to high standards and constantly seek improvement, your employees will be inspired to do the same.

2. **Empower Your Team:** Give your team the tools, training, and autonomy to succeed. When people feel empowered, they take ownership of their work and are motivated to contribute to the company's success.

3. **Foster Collaboration:** Encourage cross-functional teamwork. Excellence thrives in environments where diverse perspectives come together to solve problems and innovate.

4. **Recognize Achievements:** Celebrate the small wins as much as the big ones. Recognition and praise for effort and results foster a positive, high-performing work environment.

5. **Provide Growth Opportunities:** Encourage your team to continuously learn and improve. Offer professional development programs, mentorship opportunities, and challenges that help them grow.

Defining Success in the Pursuit of Excellence

Success in the pursuit of excellence is not solely about financial outcomes or accolades. It's about alignment between your personal values, your business goals, and the impact you have on your team and customers. A successful CEO must define what excellence looks like for both themselves and their organization.

How to Define Success:

1. **Personal Fulfilment:** Success should bring you a sense of fulfilment, not just external validation. When you feel you are growing and learning, you are on the path to true success.

2. **Positive Impact on Others:** Evaluate success based on how it benefits your team, customers, and community. A successful CEO creates an environment where others can thrive.

3. **Sustainable Growth:** Success is not just short-term achievements but long-term sustainability. It's about building a business that thrives and evolves over time.

4. **Continuous Learning:** Success is measured by your ability to learn from your mistakes and continue to improve.

Practical Steps to Pursue Excellence in Your Life and Company

1. **Set Clear, SMART Goals:** Begin by setting specific, measurable, achievable, relevant, and time-bound goals that align with your personal and company vision.

2. **Hold Yourself Accountable:** Regularly track your progress and take responsibility for both your successes and failures. Use a mentor or coach to stay accountable.

3. **Lead with Purpose:** Cultivate a culture of excellence by modelling high standards and encouraging growth and empowerment within your team.

213

4. **Celebrate Wins:** Recognize achievements—big and small. This creates a sense of pride and reinforces the company's commitment to excellence.

5. **Create Feedback Loops:** Seek feedback from your team and peers to identify areas for improvement. Use this feedback to continuously refine your strategies and goals.

Case Study: Howard Schultz and the Pursuit of Excellence at Starbucks

Howard Schultz, the former CEO of Starbucks, provides a powerful example of the pursuit of excellence in leadership. Schultz joined Starbucks when it was a small regional coffee company and turned it into a global brand with over 30,000 stores worldwide. His pursuit of excellence was evident not only in the company's products but in its culture.

Schultz had a vision of creating a "third place" between home and work where people could relax and enjoy high-quality coffee. But he didn't stop there—he implemented excellence in every aspect of the company, from the quality of coffee beans to the customer experience. Schultz set high standards for employees, offering benefits and stock options even for part-time workers, which was unheard of in the industry at the time.

His commitment to excellence was also evident in his approach to leadership. Schultz believed in transparency and accountability, often visiting stores to meet with employees and customers to understand their needs. His leadership was marked by his pursuit of personal and professional growth, continuously challenging himself and his company to reach new heights.

Under Schultz's leadership, Starbucks didn't just succeed—it became a global symbol of quality and customer service, all thanks to a relentless pursuit of excellence that permeated every level of the business.

Conclusion

The pursuit of excellence is at the heart of every successful CEO's journey. It requires vision, discipline, and an unwavering commitment to continuous improvement. By setting SMART goals, holding yourself accountable, building a culture of excellence, and defining success on your own terms, you'll create a company that thrives and delivers exceptional results. Remember, excellence is not a destination—it's a way of life that propels you, your team, and your business forward.

25

The Journey Continues

The forward journey is more than just the roadmap of your career—it's about preparing for the next phase of leadership, adapting to change, and positioning yourself and your company for future success. While the present requires you to manage daily operations and tackle immediate challenges, your forward journey is about vision, foresight, and long-term impact. It's about the decisions you make today that shape the trajectory of tomorrow.

In this chapter, we'll explore what the forward journey for a successful CEO looks like, how to achieve it, and the mindset required to embrace it. We'll also discuss the future landscape of leadership and provide practical steps for you to plan and navigate your own future journey as a CEO.

What the Forward Journey Looks Like

The forward journey for a CEO is a path of continuous growth and evolution. It goes beyond merely climbing the corporate ladder—it's about understanding the broader business environment, predicting industry trends, and positioning your company for long-term success. It is a journey of leadership refinement, personal development, and creating lasting legacies.

Key Elements of the Forward Journey:

1. **Visionary Leadership:** As a successful CEO, you must constantly look ahead and anticipate the future of your company, industry, and the world at large. This involves being able to adjust your vision to align with the times while staying true to the company's core values.

2. **Adaptability:** The business landscape is always shifting. Technological advances, economic shifts, and global challenges mean that CEOs need to

be adaptable. The ability to pivot and adjust the course of the company will define your forward journey.

3. **Long-Term Strategy:** Successful CEOs don't just focus on the next quarter—they think about the next decade. The forward journey involves developing sustainable growth strategies that ensure the company thrives long into the future.

4. **Innovation:** To move forward, CEOs must encourage innovation—not only in products or services but in processes, culture, and business models. This innovation helps the company evolve and stay ahead of the competition.

5. **Personal Growth and Legacy:** The forward journey is also about growing as a person and a leader. It's about refining your skills, broadening your knowledge, and shaping a legacy that reflects your values and achievements.

How to Achieve the Forward Journey

Achieving the forward journey requires a deliberate, thoughtful approach. Here are some of the most important elements to focus on as you move forward in your career:

1. Develop a Clear Vision for the Future

A key part of your forward journey is having a clear, compelling vision of where you want your company to be in the future. This vision should be long-term and inspiring, setting a direction for the company's growth, innovation, and impact.

Practical Steps to Develop Your Vision:

- **Conduct Market Research:** Understand emerging trends and potential disruptions in your industry.

- **Involve Your Team:** A strong vision should involve your leadership team. Work with them to develop a collective understanding of where the company is heading.

- **Set Clear Milestones:** Break down your long-term vision into achievable milestones to help guide the company over time.

- **Stay Agile:** Be open to adjusting the vision as new information and changes arise.

2. Build a Strong, Adaptive Company Culture

A forward-thinking CEO needs to create an environment that embraces change. Building a company culture that values adaptability, learning, and innovation ensures that your team is prepared for whatever challenges may come.

Practical Steps to Build a Strong Culture:

- **Encourage Open Communication:** Foster an environment where team members can express ideas and share feedback freely.

- **Promote Continuous Learning:** Invest in training programs, development workshops, and opportunities for employees to upskill.

- **Emphasize Collaboration:** Encourage cross-functional teamwork to solve problems and create innovative solutions.

3. Stay Ahead with Technology and Innovation

The forward journey of a successful CEO is intrinsically linked to staying at the cutting edge of technological advancements. Technology will continue to shape industries, and embracing innovation will be key to staying competitive.

Practical Steps to Embrace Technology:

- **Invest in R&D:** Ensure that your company is investing in research and development to stay ahead of market demands.

- **Adopt Emerging Technologies:** Explore new technologies like artificial intelligence, automation, and data analytics to improve operations and create better products.

- **Foster a Culture of Innovation:** Encourage employees to experiment with new ideas and approaches to drive the company forward.

4. Focus on Long-Term Growth, Not Short-Term Gains

While short-term goals are important, the forward journey for a successful CEO focuses on long-term growth. Whether it's scaling the business, diversifying products, or entering new markets, the CEO's role is to ensure that the company is set up for sustained success.

Practical Steps for Long-Term Growth:

- **Diversify Revenue Streams:** Look for opportunities to expand into new markets or offer complementary products.

- **Develop Strategic Partnerships:** Build relationships with other companies that can help drive mutual growth.

- **Measure Long-Term Performance:** Use long-term key performance indicators (KPIs) to measure growth, including customer retention, brand loyalty, and market share.

5. Invest in Personal Leadership Development

The forward journey isn't just about developing the company—it's about developing yourself as a leader. The best CEOs continuously work on their leadership skills, from communication to decision-making, and from emotional intelligence to vision casting.

Practical Steps for Personal Development:

- **Seek Mentorship:** Identify experienced leaders who can guide you through challenges and help you grow as a CEO.

- **Practice Self-Reflection:** Regularly assess your performance, leadership style, and areas for improvement.

- **Invest in Executive Education:** Attend leadership seminars, workshops, and programs that help you sharpen your skills and stay updated on new leadership trends.

The Future Journey: What Will It Embrace?

The future of leadership will be shaped by new technologies, shifting societal values, and an increasingly globalized and interconnected world. The forward journey will embrace a future where CEOs are not only business leaders but also ethical stewards, advocates for diversity, equity, and inclusion, and champions of sustainability.

Some key elements the future journey will embrace:

- **Sustainability:** Future CEOs will be responsible for leading organizations that prioritize environmental sustainability and social responsibility.

- **Global Perspective:** CEOs will need to manage companies that operate on a global scale, requiring a deep understanding of international markets and cultural diversity.

- **Technological Integration:** With technology playing a larger role in all industries, future CEOs will need to be tech-savvy and adaptable to leverage new innovations.

- **Inclusive Leadership:** As diversity, equity, and inclusion continue to be a priority, future leaders will need to create environments where everyone has an opportunity to succeed.

Real-Life Case Study: Satya Nadella and Microsoft's Forward Journey

When Satya Nadella became CEO of Microsoft in 2014, the company was facing challenges in staying relevant in a rapidly changing tech landscape. Nadella's forward-thinking leadership transformed Microsoft into a company that not only embraced new technologies like cloud computing and artificial intelligence but also fostered a culture of innovation and inclusivity.

Nadella's first move was to shift the company's focus from just products to services and cloud computing, an area where Microsoft was lagging behind competitors like Amazon and Google. He prioritized long-term growth by refocusing on core competencies and expanding into new markets. Under Nadella's leadership, Microsoft's cloud business, Azure, became a major revenue driver.

One of Nadella's key contributions was his emphasis on empathy and emotional intelligence in leadership. He encouraged a growth mindset within the company and led by example, focusing on personal development and self-improvement. He built an inclusive culture where diversity and collaboration were seen as essential to innovation.

As a result of these forward-thinking strategies, Microsoft's market value soared, and the company became a leader in the cloud computing and AI spaces. Nadella's visionary approach and ability to embrace change ensured that Microsoft's journey moved forward with a renewed sense of purpose and innovation.

Conclusion

The forward journey for a successful CEO is one that demands vision, adaptability, and a deep commitment to long-term growth. By setting clear goals, embracing innovation, fostering a strong company culture, and continuously developing as a leader, you can navigate the ever-changing business landscape and secure your company's future. As you move forward, remember that the journey is not just about achieving success—it's about shaping a lasting legacy and making an impact for years to come.

Conclusion

As you reach the end of *Modern CEO Toolkit*, I hope you've gained valuable insights and actionable strategies that will empower you to become a more effective, resilient, and visionary leader. Being a CEO in today's world is not just about making the right decisions for your company's success—it's about shaping a culture of growth, adaptability, and continuous improvement. It's about leading with integrity, fostering strong relationships, and embracing the constant changes that come with the modern business landscape.

Throughout this book, we've covered a broad spectrum of essential topics, from emotional intelligence and strategic visioning, to mentorship and the pursuit of excellence. Each of these lessons is a piece of the larger puzzle that will help you not only lead effectively, but inspire others to do the same. The tools and frameworks shared here are designed to give you the confidence and the clarity needed to navigate the complexities of leadership, while ensuring you build a business that's both sustainable and future-ready.

But leadership is a lifelong journey. There is no final destination, only continuous growth and adaptation. As you apply these lessons, remember that success is not defined by a single moment, but by your ability to evolve, learn from your experiences, and stay focused on your long-term vision.

In your role as CEO, you will face challenges, make tough decisions, and encounter moments of uncertainty. But by building a strong foundation of resilience, emotional intelligence, and a relentless commitment to excellence, you can navigate any obstacle and turn challenges into opportunities for growth.

I encourage you to take the insights from this book and apply them in your daily leadership practice. Lead with purpose, embrace change, and above all, stay true to the values that define you as a leader. Your journey as a CEO is unique, and the lessons you've learned here will serve as a guide to not only achieve success but to leave a lasting impact on your company, your team, and the world around you.

The road ahead is yours to shape. Now, with the lessons you've gained, take the next step in your leadership journey and lead your organization toward new heights.

Thank you for taking this journey with me.

References

L isted below are a number of references used to write this book as well as my personal experience.

1. Goleman, D. (1995). *Emotional Intelligence: Why It Can Matter More Than IQ*. Bantam.
    A foundational book that explores the concept of emotional intelligence and its impact on leadership and decision-making, offering insights into how CEOs can harness emotional intelligence to improve their effectiveness.

2. Collins, J. (2001). *Good to Great: Why Some Companies Make the Leap... and Others Don't*. HarperBusiness.

    This book provides valuable lessons on leadership and business excellence, showing how CEOs can drive companies to long-term success through disciplined leadership and a focus on the right people and strategy.

3. Kotter, J. P. (1996). *Leading Change*. Harvard Business Press. A must-read for understanding how effective CEOs manage organizational change. Kotter outlines a step-by-step process for leading successful transformations that will be essential for CEOs in today's rapidly changing business landscape.

4. Lencioni, P. (2002). *The Five Dysfunctions of a Team: A Leadership Fable*. Jossey-Bass.
    Lencioni's work offers insights into how CEOs can build high-performance teams by understanding common dysfunctions that impede team success, and provides actionable steps for fostering collaboration and trust within teams.

5. Grant, A. (2013). *Give and Take: A Revolutionary Approach to Success*. Viking. Grant explores the importance of networking, mentorship, and creating value for others, showing how CEOs can leverage these principles to foster long-term business growth and personal success.

6. Schein, E. H. (2010). *Organizational Culture and Leadership*. Jossey-Bass. This book examines how CEOs can shape organizational culture to drive corporate success, emphasizing the importance of leadership in fostering an ethical and high-performance workplace.

7. Christensen, C. M. (1997). *The Innovator's Dilemma: When New Technologies Cause Great Firms to Fail*. Harvard Business Review Press. Christensen's book is essential for understanding how CEOs can manage innovation and stay ahead of industry disruptions. It teaches how to balance sustaining innovations wit disruptive ones, which is crucial for a CEO's long-term strategic vision.

These references provide a strong foundation for anyone looking to improve their leadership skills, build successful teams, and navigate the complexities of modern business.

www.ingramcontent.com/pod-product-compliance
Lightning Source LLC
Chambersburg PA
CBHW030505210326
41597CB00013B/803